NATURAL SATELLITES

THE BOOK OF MOONS

RON MILLER

TWENTY-FIRST CENTURY BOOKS / MINNEAPOLIS

THIS BOOK IS DEDICATED TO LUCA SCELFO CAVOLI

Twenty-First Century Books™
An imprint of Lerner Publishing Group, Inc.
241 First Avenue North
Minneapolis, MN 55401 USA

For reading levels and more information, look up this title at www.lernerbooks.com.

Main body text set in Adobe Garamond Pro.
Typeface provided by Adobe Systems.

Library of Congress Cataloging-in-Publication Data

Names: Miller, Ron, 1947– author, illustrator.
Title: Natural satellites: the book of moons / Ron Miller.
Description: Minneapolis, MN: Twenty-First Century Books, [2021] | Includes
    bibliographical references and index. | Audience: Ages 13–18 | Audience: Grades 10–12
    | Summary: The moons of our solar system feature extreme and potentially life-hosting
    environments. This book delves into the science behind the fascinating properties of
    various moons and explains why astronomers search for life on moons— Provided by
    publisher.
Identifiers: LCCN 2020009972 (print) | LCCN 2020009973 (ebook) | ISBN
    9781728419435 (library binding) | ISBN 9781728419442 (ebook)
Subjects: LCSH: Satellites—Juvenile literature. | Outer planets—Satellites—Juvenile
    literature.
Classification: LCC QB401.5 .M555 2021 (print) | LCC QB401.5 (ebook) | DDC
    523.9/8—dc23

LC record available at https://lccn.loc.gov/2020009972
LC ebook record available at https://lccn.loc.gov/2020009973

Manufactured in the United States of America
1-49062-49265-11/2/2020

TABLE OF CONTENTS

INTRODUCTION

It's hard to imagine the night sky without the Moon. Next to the sun, our moon is the largest, brightest object in the sky. Sometimes the Moon is as big, round, and brilliant as a spotlight, and sometimes it is a thin crescent, like a pale eyelash. Sometimes it is not even visible in the night sky but appears during the day. With a small telescope or even a pair of binoculars, we can explore the side of the Moon that faces Earth. We can see craters, vast plains, valleys, and mountains. It sometimes looks as if we could reach out and touch it.

Scientists have done just that. Spacecraft have photographed and mapped virtually every square foot of the Moon, probes and rovers have explored it, and astronauts have walked on it and even brought back samples of its surface. Astronauts also brought back pictures of the Moon, showing a place that is as stark as a desert but also beautiful.

Earth's moon is far from alone. Most of our neighbors in the solar system—Jupiter, Saturn, Uranus, Neptune, and Pluto—have multiple moons that are very different from Earth's moon. In fact, Mercury and Venus are the only planets with no moons.

Despite how much we have explored our own moon, it wasn't until the late twentieth century that astronomers realized how diverse and interesting the other moons of the solar system really are. Previously, scientists had largely ignored the satellites orbiting other planets. Many of these moons are small, and they are all very distant, making them difficult to study. For example, Titan, the largest moon of Saturn and the second-largest moon in the solar system, was discovered by Christiaan Huygens in 1655, but no one knew that it had an atmosphere until 1944. Until the 1970s, all that any astronomer could tell you about any of the solar system's moons was their approximate size.

This changed when spacecraft made the first close-up flybys of many of the moons. The *Voyager 1* and *Voyager 2* spacecraft launched in 1977. Two years later, they arrived at Jupiter. For the first time, astronomers got a close look at moons Galileo had discovered more than three hundred years earlier. The moons were no longer tiny specks in a telescope but real worlds with their own histories, geologies, and landscapes. The *Voyager* spacecraft continued on to Saturn, where in 1980 and 1981 they took the first close-up photos of many of that planet's moons, including mysterious, cloud-shrouded Titan. While *Voyager 1* didn't travel past any other planets, *Voyager 2* flew by Uranus in 1986 and Neptune in 1989, collecting photos of many of those planets' moons.

Astronomers discovered that every moon in the solar system had its own set of unique features. While the primary goal of the two spacecraft had been to explore Jupiter, Saturn, Uranus, and Neptune, some of the biggest surprises, from fiery volcanoes to enormous canyons to geysers that shoot snowy ice crystals hundreds of miles

EARTH

Moon

MARS

Phobos

Deimos

JUPITER

Io

Europa

Ganymede

Callisto

SATURN

Mimas

Enceladus

Tethys

Dione

Rhea

Titan

Hyperion

Iapetus

Phoebe

The major moons of the
solar system, to scale

URANUS

Puck

Miranda

Ariel

Umbriel

Titania

Oberon

NEPTUNE

Proteus

Triton

Nereid

PLUTO

Charon

into the sky, were found on the planets' moons. Such features, once relegated to the realm of fantasy, proved that the moons were far from boring, and some of them were *active*. Things were going on. These discoveries changed everything. Astronomers looked on the moons of the solar system with newly opened eyes. Instead of being footnotes, the moons became objects of special interest.

In the decades following the *Voyager* discoveries, many other spacecraft have visited some of the solar system's moons, and scientists plan to send dedicated orbiters and landers to some moons. Their goal is to find out how the moons came into existence, why they look the way they do, what they might tell us about the birth of the solar system, and perhaps even whether they harbor life. And in the future, the solar system's moons may serve as way stations on the road to humankind's exploration of space. There is, after all, a moon where it rains rocket fuel. In light of so many unanswered questions and wonderful possibilities, astronomers are finally giving the moons the attention they are due.

1

THE BIRTH OF THE SOLAR SYSTEM

The word *planet* comes from a Greek word meaning "wanderer." Originally, it referred to five bright stars in the night sky that did something unusual. Unlike the thousands of other stars in the sky, which always remained in the same place, the planets moved around quite a bit. No one knew why they did this, but observers assumed there must be something very special about them. To recognize this, the ancient Romans named them after their gods: Mercury, Venus, Mars, Jupiter, and Saturn.

For thousands of years, that was what the word *planet* meant: a special kind of moving star. That changed during the winter of 1610 when the Italian scientist Galileo Galilei became the first person to turn a telescope toward the night sky. He saw that Venus and Mercury showed phases like the Moon, appearing at times like a crescent and at other times like a ball, and Jupiter seemed to be circled by four tiny moons of its own, just as Earth is circled by its moon. And as for Earth's moon, once thought to be a perfectly smooth sphere, Galileo found it to be "full of inequalities, uneven, full of hollows and protuberances, just like the surface of the Earth itself, which is varied everywhere by lofty mountains and deep valleys."

Scientists soon realized that Earth was just one member of a system of worlds that all orbited the sun: the solar system (named for Sol, Latin for "sun"). People developed many theories about the origin of the solar system and its planets. One of the earliest scientific theories was published in 1749 by the French naturalist Georges-Louis Leclerc. Leclerc suggested that a giant comet had once collided with the sun. This collision blew masses of material off the sun that eventually became the planets. In 1755 philosopher Immanuel Kant said that the sun and planets formed from a vast, nebulous cloud of dust and gas billions of miles in diameter, a theory that was further developed by mathematician and philosopher Pierre-Simon Laplace in 1796. As the cloud contracted under its own gravity, the theory went, the sun formed at the center. Meanwhile, the cloud began to rotate, which caused it to flatten out into a ring or series of rings. The planets formed within these rings, and their moons formed around them the same way the planets had formed around the sun.

Laplace's idea was severely criticized. Some, such as Sir David Brewster, who was both a scientist and an official in his church, thought that the theory was heresy since it suggested a natural origin for Earth instead of the one given by the Bible. Others, such as the astronomer Richard Proctor, attacked the theory on mathematical grounds, offering proofs that Laplace's nebula wouldn't act as Laplace had described it.

In 1905 Thomas C. Chamberlin, a geologist, and Forest Ray Moulton, an astronomer, published a radical new theory. They suggested that the solar system was the result of a near collision of the sun with an enormous star. As the star sideswiped the sun, its tremendous gravitation ripped a huge jet of gas from our star. This left a spiraling swarm of particles that eventually coalesced into the planets. Since two stars almost never pass by each other so closely, this theory suggested that the creation of solar systems was a rare event.

From 1914 to 1916, Sir James Jeans and Sir Harold Jeffreys modified Chamberlin and Moulton's idea to come up with their tidal theory. It too proposed a near miss by a wandering star, but it suggested that the star's gravity created a huge bulge in the sun, which broke away to form the planets. Their theory, like those theories before it, contributed to the present view of how all solar systems, including our own, were formed.

FROM PROTOSTAR TO SOLAR SYSTEM

Scientists currently believe that the sun and planets formed about 4.5 billion years ago from an enormous cloud of dust and gas. The cloud was about 65 light-years across, about one hundred thousand times the distance from the sun to Pluto.

Eventually, the cloud began to collapse. Scientists aren't sure how the collapse began, but many think it was triggered by the shock wave from a nearby exploding star. As the shock wave moved through the cloud, individual molecules of gas and particles of dust moved closer together. Their mutual gravitational attraction increased, causing the contraction to continue. Once this process began, the cloud shrank to a millionth of its original size over the course of a few million years—quick in astronomical times.

The sun pushed much of the solar system's water to the outer reaches of the system, where the water froze into the icy bodies of the Kuiper Belt. These icy bodies would knock each other out of orbit, becoming comets that crashed into Earth and delivered water to our planet.

As the center of the cloud became denser, its gravity increased, causing it to collapse even further. Just as the air in a car tire will heat up as it is compressed, the core of the dust cloud began to heat up. Soon it was glowing a dull red within the dark cloud. The cloud had become a protostar.

Eventually—perhaps only a hundred thousand years after the cloud first began to condense—the core became dense and hot enough to trigger a nuclear reaction. When this happened, the protostar became a star. The nuclear reaction increased the amount of heat coming out of the star, creating an outward pressure that resisted the collapsing dust and gas. The collapse came to a halt.

Within the cloud surrounding the protostar, tiny particles of dust collided and stuck together, forming little clumps of material. As these clumps, called planetesimals, grew in size, they attracted more particles. And the larger they got, the more particles they attracted in a process called accretion. These clumps of dust gradually grew to the size of asteroids. The growth, from the size of a pinhead to the size of a mountain, may have taken only one hundred thousand years or so. Then the accretion began to slow down. The original cloud of dust and gas was being used up, and the cloud was growing thin.

As the planetesimals grew larger, they moved faster, and the collisions between them became more violent. Instead of sticking together when they impacted, some of them shattered into pieces. The few planetesimals large enough to survive these collisions grew even larger, devouring not only the debris from collisions but every smaller object that crossed their paths.

Scientists think it may have taken as few as forty million years for Earth to grow from a speck of dust to an object nearly its present size. Within this time, a giant, dark, cold cloud of dust and gas had transformed itself into a solar system, with a bright, warm sun in its center and a family of planets.

THE BIRTH OF MOONS

Each planet began as a dense knot of gas and dust within the larger cloud surrounding the infant sun. As a planet slowly formed, some of the dust and gas surrounding it formed even smaller lumps. These lumps accreted material of their own as they orbited the baby planets, eventually becoming moons.

Not every planet had a moon. Neither Mercury nor Venus have one. Astronomers think the reason might be their closeness to the sun. Not only did the sun consume any extra available material, but heat and radiation pressure also pushed dust and gas to the outer reaches of the solar system. However, some scientists think that Venus may have once had a moon, but tremendous impacts either destroyed the moon or flung the moon away.

The heat also kept lighter materials such as ice from forming, and the radiation pressure blew dust and gas away like the breeze from a giant fan. The result was that the planets closest to the sun (Mercury, Venus, Earth, and Mars) are all made of rock and metal, while planets much farther away from the sun (Jupiter, Saturn, Uranus, and Neptune) are made mostly of ice and cold gases. A similar process affected the formation of moons. When Jupiter was very young, for example, it was a hot ball of gas. Its heat prevented icy moons from forming nearby, just as the sun prevented icy worlds from forming near it. So Jupiter's nearest moons tend to be rocky, and those farther away from the planet are icier (except for its captured asteroid moons).

But not every moon in the solar system formed in this way. The early solar system was filled with debris that the forming planets had not swept up. Millions of leftover planetesimals, made mostly of rock and metal, filled the asteroid belt, a region between Mars and Jupiter. In the orbit of the dwarf planet Pluto, icy bodies—too far away to have been affected by the sun's radiation—formed a band called the Kuiper Belt.

While many of the solar system's planetesimals orbited the sun in neat, nearly circular paths that kept them at a safe distance from their neighbors, others had wildly eccentric orbits and sometimes collided with planets or moons. More often than not, these collisions produced nothing more than a crater, like the thousands that pockmark our moon. Sometimes, though, a collision was big enough to nearly destroy a planet. In such a collision, the huge amount of molten material blown

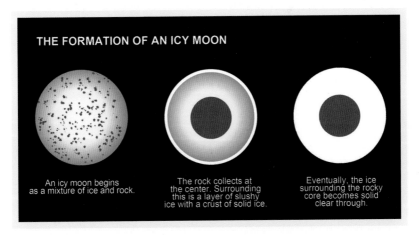

THE FORMATION OF AN ICY MOON

An icy moon begins as a mixture of ice and rock.

The rock collects at the center. Surrounding this is a layer of slushy ice with a crust of solid ice.

Eventually, the ice surrounding the rocky core becomes solid clear through.

Water is very abundant in the solar system, but most of it is frozen. The icy moons of the solar system contain some of this ice in thick layers on top of a rocky core.

into space might wind up becoming a moon. Our own moon was probably created this way, as was Pluto's largest moon, Charon.

Other times a planetesimal avoided colliding with a planet but instead came so close that it was captured by the planet's gravity. It would go into orbit around the planet, becoming a moon. This was probably the origin of Mars's two small moons, as well as many of the outer moons of Jupiter and Saturn.

Eventually, all of the extra planetesimals ended up in safe orbits around the sun, were swept up in collisions, or became moons, producing a relatively tidy solar system.

2

WHAT *IS* A MOON?

Regardless of size, any object that orbits a planet, dwarf planet, or asteroid is a moon. Some moons in our solar system are bigger than the planet Mercury, while others are so small that you might be able to hold them in your hand. Our own moon is a quarter of the size of Earth and one of the largest solar system moons relative to its planet.

The scientific term for an orbiting body is *satellite*, which comes from a Latin word meaning "companion." The Moon is Earth's satellite, and Earth is the sun's satellite. Ever since 1957, when the first human-made satellite, *Sputnik*, was launched into orbit around Earth, a distinction had to be made between natural satellites, such as Earth's moon or the moons of Mars and Jupiter, and artificial satellites, such as the International Space Station.

CANNONBALLS AND MOONS

People knew for many centuries that the Moon circles Earth. Yet no one knew how or why it did this until Sir Isaac Newton (1643–1727), an English mathematician and scientist, studied the subject. Newton knew that anything unsupported will fall to the ground. If you let go of this book, it will drop to the floor. Newton asked an interesting question: If anything unsupported will fall to Earth, what keeps the Moon up in the sky? Why doesn't it fall just as the book does? Newton published his answer in a book, *Philosophiae Naturalis Principia Mathematica*—the *Principia* for short.

To explain why the Moon never falls to Earth, Newton used the example of a projectile fired from a cannon. If there were no force of gravity, he wrote, the cannonball would not fall toward Earth.

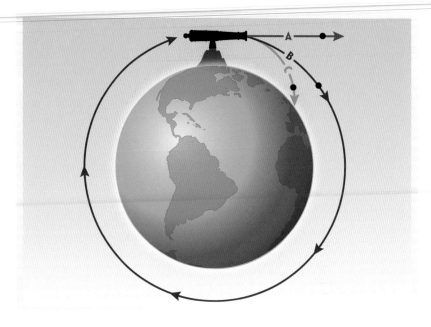

A cannonball fired at just the right velocity will orbit around Earth (B). If the velocity is too low, gravity will pull the cannonball to the ground (C). If the velocity is too high, the cannonball will escape Earth entirely (A).

It would shoot away from the planet in a straight line. But because gravity exists, the cannonball is pulled toward Earth. Instead of traveling in a straight line, its path becomes a curve that eventually meets the surface of Earth. A cannonball shot from the top of a mountain, Newton said, might travel only a few miles before it hits the ground. But if the cannon were powerful enough, the curved path of the cannonball would be the same as the curvature of the planet beneath it. The cannonball would never hit the ground but would keep circling the planet forever. It would be in orbit.

ISAAC NEWTON

Sir Isaac Newton (1643–1727) was an English physicist, mathematician, astronomer, and natural philosopher. Many historians and scientists consider him to be one of the greatest scientists who ever lived. In *Philosophiae Naturalis Principia Mathematica*, Newton described the laws by which gravitation affects everything from apples to planets. He was the first to show that the motion of objects on Earth and the motion of the planets and their moons are all governed by these three basic laws, now known as Newton's laws of motion:

1. **The law of inertia.** An object at rest remains at rest unless an outside force acts on it. An object in motion continues in motion at the same speed and in the same direction unless an outside force acts on it. So an object tends to keep doing what it is already doing.
2. **The law of force.** When a force acts on an object, it accelerates (changes the speed and direction of) the object. The greater the object's mass, the greater the force needed to accelerate it. So the heavier an object is, the harder it is to move.
3. **The law of momentum.** For every action, there is an equal and opposite reaction.

The same is true for Earth's moon. The Moon really *is* falling toward Earth, but Earth is never there to meet it because its surface curves away.

The same laws that govern the orbit of our Moon also apply to every other moon in the solar system, no matter where it is, how big or small it is, or what planet it orbits.

OUR MOON IS SPECIAL

Despite following the same orbital laws, Earth's moon is very different from most of the other moons in the solar system. For example, the Moon is large relative to Earth, while most other moons in the solar system are small relative to the planets they orbit. Our moon has a unique origin compared to those of the other moons in the solar system and is the only celestial object, besides Earth, that humans have set foot on.

The nearside of the Moon, as photographed by NASA's *Lunar Reconnaissance Orbiter*, with its dark maria clearly visible.

FACTS ABOUT THE MOON

Diameter: 2,160 miles (3,476 km)

Distance from Earth: 238,855 miles (384,400 km)

Length of day: 27.3 days

Length of time to orbit Earth: 27.3 days

Although the Moon is visible almost every night to everyone on Earth, for thousands of years no one knew that the Moon was actually a place. It was, to many ancient peoples, only a beautiful bright light in the sky, mysteriously changing shape throughout the month. Some of the indigenous peoples of South America believed that the sun was a man and that the Moon was his wife. In central India and northern China, ancient peoples worshipped the sun and Moon as gods, while the Polynesians believed that the Moon was the heavenly abode of chieftains. Several Native American tribes had stories about the Moon and the heroes and gods who might live there. Early observers wondered about the dusky markings on the Moon. A few ancient Greek philosophers thought that the Moon might have fields, valleys, and mountains like those on Earth, perhaps even with towns, people, and animals.

While many observers around the world studied the Moon closely, they all faced one key obstacle: all their observations had to be done with the naked eye. Since the Moon doesn't appear much larger than a dime held at arm's length, they struggled to make out any details beyond tantalizingly vague areas of shadow and lightness.

This changed when the telescope was invented in the Netherlands in the early seventeenth century. Militaries, navies, and ship captains immediately adopted the tool, but hardly anyone thought of turning a telescope toward the sky until Galileo decided to try it. From fall

1609 to early spring 1610, Galileo began observing the night sky with a telescope he built. It was no more powerful than a modern pair of small, inexpensive binoculars. But it revealed things no one had ever expected to see.

What Galileo learned on those cold nights forever changed how we look at Earth and the heavens. He saw that the Moon is not made of some pure, unearthly, celestial substance but is covered with mountains and craters. Its appearance seemed familiar. The Moon was, Galileo wrote, "not smooth, uniform, and precisely spherical as a great number of philosophers believe it (and the other heavenly bodies) to be, but is uneven, rough, and full of cavities and prominences, being not unlike the face of the earth." As Galileo watched the shadows change on the Moon's surface, he realized that the Moon's light was actually reflected sunlight. It had no light of its own.

Other scientists quickly confirmed Galileo's findings, including that the Moon was actually an object. Almost literally overnight, Galileo changed humankind's perception of the Moon.

HOW THE MOON GOT ITS NAME

For thousands of years, no one knew that there were any other moons than the one they saw in the sky. It was *the* Moon, and that was that. The word *moon* itself comes from Old English and is related to Latin words meaning "month" and "to measure"—both referring to how people were able to keep track of the passage of time by the regular changing of the Moon's phases. When Galileo discovered, in 1610, that other planets also had objects orbiting them, it seemed natural to refer to these objects as moons too. So Earth has a moon called the Moon, while the other planets have moons with names of their own.

THE ORIGIN OF THE MOON

When the astronauts from NASA's Apollo space program (1969–1972) brought back samples of the lunar surface, scientists learned exactly what the Moon is made of and how old it is. The Moon is nearly the same age as Earth and formed of almost exactly the same materials. This information helped shape the newest theory about how the Moon came to exist.

One hundred million years after the planets began to form in the protoplanetary disk, the young Earth was only just beginning to cool down after its formation. Its surface was still molten, a global sea of red-hot rock.

The rest of the solar system was filled with the leftover debris of its formation. Millions of rocky bodies from the size of dust grains and boulders to small planets were constantly colliding with one another and with the newly formed planets. Earth caught its share of them. Most of these colliding bodies were relatively small: meteors and asteroids that were at most only a few miles wide. But one roaming body was bigger than all the rest—almost as big as the planet Mars— and it ran directly into Earth. The result was catastrophic. The young Earth was almost completely destroyed, turned into a huge, red-hot, doughnut-shaped cloud of molten rock called a synestia. At the center was a glob of semisolid rock and metal that was a combination of Earth and the impactor. Soon the liquid rock in the cloud began to condense at the center of the synestia. As the cloud slowly cooled, more rock condensed—like raindrops—and collected at the center, causing the molten glob that was already there to become larger and larger, and Earth began to regrow.

Meanwhile, some of the droplets in the synestia clustered to form little moonlets. One of these, slightly larger than the rest, acted as a kind of seed around which ever more moonlets gathered. It eventually became our moon. Amazingly, the moon's formation may have taken less than a hundred years.

While Earth—or an early version of Earth—existed *before* the dramatic impact that created the Moon, the planet took longer to reform from the synestia than the Moon did. This means that the Moon formed before Earth as we know it.

THE MODERN MOON

Other than collecting thousands of craters—the result of the impact of meteors and asteroids—the Moon has changed very little in the four billion years since its creation. When the earliest ancestors of modern humans looked up at the night sky, they saw essentially the same moon you see today. It is certainly the most familiar of all our neighbors in space. Since the same side of the Moon always faces Earth, many people assume that the Moon does not rotate on its axis, but it does. This rotation allows it to always keep one side toward Earth.

You can see for yourself why this is true. Put a chair in the middle of a room. Walk in a circle around the chair, always facing it. When you get back to where you started, you will have also faced all four walls of the room. You could not have done this if you had not made one rotation on your axis while you made one revolution around the chair.

Another misconception about the Moon is that it has a permanent dark side that can never be seen from Earth. Although the side of the

A MOON BY ANY OTHER NAME

The ancient Greeks named the Moon after the goddess of the Moon, Selene. The name appears in the English word for the study of the Moon: *selenography*. The ancient Romans called the Moon Luna, which shows up in modern usage when we talk about lunar explorers or lunar craters. Contemporary English's word *moon* derives from Old English, but the Moon has very different names in other languages. In French, the Moon is Lune, in Turkish it is Ay, and in Swahili it is Mwezi.

In naming the other moons of the solar system, astronomers went back to the Greek and Roman tradition of naming objects in the sky after gods and goddesses. Mars was the Roman god of war, so astronomers named its two moons Phobos (fear) and Deimos (terror), the companions of war. The four largest moons of Jupiter—Io, Europa, Callisto, and Ganymede—were named by German astronomer Simon Marius (1573–1625) shortly after their discovery. These were the names of some of the lovers of the god Jupiter in Roman mythology. Galileo wanted to call them the Medicean stars in honor of his patron, Cosimo de' Medici, but few adopted this terminology. Astronomers have maintained Marius's theme by naming most of Jupiter's other moons after other lovers or descendants of Jupiter.

Saturn's largest moon, Titan, was named for its size after the race of giants, known as the Titans, in Roman mythology. Many of Saturn's smaller moons have been named after other Titans and Titanesses in Roman mythology, including Iapetus, Rhea, and Dione. The moons of Uranus are named after magical characters from the plays and poems of William Shakespeare and Alexander Pope. Titania and Oberon, for instance, were the fairy queen and king in Shakespeare's *A Midsummer Night's Dream*.

Neptune was named for the Roman god of the sea. So its largest moon, Triton, was named for Neptune's son. The planet's other moons are named for other ancient Greek and Roman sea deities. Since Pluto was named for the Roman god of the underworld, its large moon, Charon, was named for the one who ferried souls across the River Styx. Pluto's other moons are also named for characters who occupied the ancient Greek and Roman underworld, such as Kerberos, the three-headed dog in Greek mythology that guarded the underworld's entrance.

Moon facing away from Earth—called the farside—can never be seen from Earth's surface, it is not always dark. As the Moon circles Earth, every part of its surface is eventually lit by the sun. This leads to the Moon's phases as seen from Earth. During the new moon—when the Moon is invisible in the night sky—the side facing us is dark, and the side facing away from Earth is lit by the sun.

A VISIT TO THE MOON

The Moon has thousands of craters, ranging from just a few feet across to up to 1,600 miles (2,575 km) wide. The impact of meteoroids and asteroids created most of these craters. Some are surrounded by streaks of bright material, or rays, that radiate out from the craters like starbursts. Scientists think the rays were created when the explosion of the impact ejected finely powdered material.

The dark patches on the Moon's surface are vast, flat plains of old lava. They are called maria (singular *mare*), from the Latin word for "sea," since Galileo thought they were bodies of water. They probably formed when huge asteroids punched through the crust of the Moon, allowing seas of molten rock to pour onto the surface. Astronomers have determined that the maria are younger, or formed more recently, than the surrounding areas because they have far fewer craters.

The Moon also has many mountain ranges. Some of these mountains are as high as any on Earth, with several rising more than 26,000 feet (7,925 m) above the surrounding plains. By comparison, Mount Everest, the highest mountain on Earth, rises 29,029 feet (8,848 m) above sea level.

One of the most prominent mountains on the Moon is Mons Pico. It is not a very high mountain—less than 7,870 feet (2,400 m) tall—but it sits all by itself in the Mare Imbrium, one of the Moon's maria. It is the lone remnant of the mountainous rim of a giant crater that was buried by the lava flow.

Meandering across the Moon's surface are sinuous valleys called

The lone peak of Mons Pico would be an impressive sight to lunar visitors.

rills that were probably formed by molten lava in much the same way that water carves out valleys on Earth. There are also high, steep cliffs, or scarps. The most famous is the Straight Wall. It is more than 68 miles (109 km) long and between 500 and 1,500 feet (150 to 450 m) high. It was created when a huge block of the lunar surface rose above the surrounding area.

The surface of the Moon is covered with a fine, powdery soil composed mostly of tiny beads of orangish glass. When meteoroid and asteroid impacts throw out millions of tons of superheated, vaporized rock, the vaporized rock condenses as it cools into countless tiny droplets of volcanic glass.

For a long time, scientists thought the surface of the Moon didn't have any water because they believed the sun would vaporize any water molecules. In 1971 the Apollo 14 mission detected water vapor on the Moon. In 2020, NASA scientists, using a special telescope carried aboard a high-flying jet aircraft, discovered water molecules on the sunlit surface of the Moon. This water may be in the form of very tiny droplets lying between grains of lunar soil that shield the droplets from the sun's energy.

Future lunar colonists would need large, easily extracted sources of water. Extracting water from the soil might be too complicated. So scientists had also wondered if there might be any large bodies of

EXPLORING THE MOON

The Moon's existence was instrumental in motivating humans to explore space. Seeing another world high above us provided the inspiration to travel away from Earth. After sending a few robotic probes to the Moon, human beings finally landed on the surface on July 20, 1969. NASA's Apollo 11 mission carried three US astronauts to the Moon: Michael Collins (b. 1930), Neil Armstrong (1930–2012), and Buzz Aldrin (b. 1930). Collins remained in orbit around the Moon in the Apollo shuttle while the other two astronauts made the descent in a small, spiderlike spacecraft called the Lunar Excursion Module. On the surface, Armstrong and Aldrin gathered rocks and samples and took photographs for more than twenty-one hours.

After Apollo 11's successful mission, five other expeditions to the Moon followed. These were a little more ambitious. Whereas the Apollo 11 astronauts didn't stray much more than a hundred feet (30 m) from the Lunar Excursion Module, other Apollo missions carried a small battery-powered car, a lunar rover, that allowed them to travel several miles from the landing site. Using the lunar rover, astronauts explored lunar maria, mountains, craters, and rills and brought back valuable information about the formation of both Earth and the Moon. The last humans to visit the Moon landed there in 1972. Due to changing priorities for space programs, no one has been back since.

liquid or frozen water somewhere on the surface of the Moon. In 2009 NASA's Moon Mineralogy Mapper (M^3)—an imaging instrument that created a detailed map of the Moon's surface—detected the presence of water at the bottom of deep craters at the lunar south pole, shielded from the sun. NASA confirmed the discovery in 2018. The water that M^3 detected is in the form of ice. Because the axis of the Moon has a very small inclination, or tilt (only 1.5 degrees, compared to Earth's 24 degrees), there are regions at the poles where the sun never rises above the rims of the deepest craters. Frozen water can exist in these regions.

Since the crater floors receive very little, if any, direct sunlight these are some of the coldest places in the entire solar system. Above some of these craters may be Peaks of Eternal Light. These hypothetical peaks would be in sunlight almost all year, while all the rest of the landscape would be in nearly perpetual darkness. Although no such peaks have been definitively observed, computer simulations have shown that some mountains near the south pole may be illuminated by the sun more than 80 percent of the year. For future space explorers, such peaks would be the ideal location for solar energy generators.

Perhaps one of the most beautiful views from the Moon would be Earth itself, which would be visible from anywhere on the nearside. Because the same side of the Moon always faces Earth, our planet would never set, always being visible in the same place in the sky. It would appear four times larger than a full moon as seen from Earth and, because of its cloud cover reflecting the sun, much brighter. As the sun slowly moves through the sky, our planet would go through phases just as the Moon does for us.

THE MOON AND LIFE ON EARTH

The Moon does more than illuminate our night skies. It has a very direct, important effect on our planet. As it orbits Earth, its gravity pulls on the oceans, causing the sea level to rise and fall in what we call tides. In astronomy, however, the term *tide* refers to any bulge caused by the gravity of an object as it pulls on another body. Tides can occur in water, ice, or even solid rock.

As the oceans are dragged over the surface of Earth by the Moon, they act as a kind of brake on Earth's rotation. Tides have been gradually slowing the spin of Earth over the billions of years since the Moon was formed. Not long after the Moon and Earth formed, Earth's day was probably only five or six hours long. Due to the drag of the tides, the rotation has been slowing down ever since, though only by a few fractions of a second every year.

ECLIPSES

As the Moon circles Earth, it occasionally passes in front of the sun, causing a solar eclipse. The sky begins to grow dark. Then brighter stars appear and the air grows cool. Birds and animals become quiet, thinking that night is falling, while nighttime insects begin chirping. As the Moon blots out the sun, the outer atmosphere of the sun, the corona, becomes visible as glowing streamers of light.

Sometimes Earth comes between the sun and the Moon, creating a lunar eclipse. When this happens, the Moon passes through the shadow of Earth and turns a deep copper color. The color is caused by sunlight that has passed through Earth's atmosphere. From the Moon, Earth would appear to be a black disk surrounded by a thin orange ring—the atmosphere of Earth illuminated from behind by the sun. This is the light from all the sunsets and sunrises on Earth at the same time.

If the Moon orbited Earth in the same plane as its orbit around the sun, we would have eclipses of the sun and Moon every month. But the Moon's orbit is tipped, so that sometimes it passes above or below Earth's shadow or above or below the sun. It is only those rare times when its orbit crosses the sun-Earth line that an eclipse can occur.

Some people call lunar eclipses "blood moons" due to the red color that the Moon takes on.

One less visible, but still very important, result of the Moon's gravitation is the steadying effect it has had on Earth's axis. If you spin a top, you can see how it wobbles around. The wobble is called precession. For a top as large as Earth, the precession takes thousands of years to occur, but it can impact a planet's climate because it changes the angle of the axis. For example, for thousands of years, the axis might be tipped at a more severe angle (more toward the sun), making the difference in seasons very extreme. But then the precession might eventually cause the axis to tilt more upright (perpendicular to the sun), making the seasonal changes less severe. The gravitational pull of the Moon prevents this precession from changing too much and too suddenly. A similar wobble has occurred on Mars. But since the planet has no large moon to steady it, the tilt of Mars's axis has changed more frequently and more severely than Earth's throughout the solar system's history. So Mars's climate has also undergone drastic changes more frequently than Earth's has. This has had a stark effect on Mars, which once had a dense atmosphere and bodies of liquid water such as lakes, seas, and rivers, but is now dry with almost no water and with only a very thin atmosphere.

TIDAL LOCKING

The Moon rotates on its axis in exactly the same amount of time it takes for the Moon to orbit Earth. This occurs because of the effect of Earth's gravity on the Moon. The Moon is not perfectly round, so Earth's gravity tugs at one side a little more than the other. Over millions of years, this has caused the Moon's rotation to gradually slow down. So the Moon always keeps one side facing our planet. Until spacecraft orbited the Moon in the 1960s, no one knew what the other side of the Moon looked like.

THE PHASES OF THE MOON

From night to night, the Moon appears to change its shape. Sometimes it's a full, round disk, while sometimes it is a thin crescent. These various shapes are the Moon's phases. As it circles Earth, the sun's light strikes the Moon from different angles. During a full moon, the Moon is on the opposite side of Earth from the sun. Full moons rise as the sun sets. During a quarter moon, the Moon, Earth, and the sun are at right angles. A quarter moon will be overhead at sunset. Many people call this phase a half moon. Astronomers call it a quarter moon because people on Earth can see only one-fourth of the entire surface of the Moon. A new moon occurs when the moon is between Earth and the sun, so the side in shadow is facing us, and we cannot see it. Between these phases are crescent moons and gibbous moons.

As seen from the Moon, Earth goes through phases too. The phases of Earth are always exactly opposite those of the Moon. During a new moon, for instance, someone on the Moon would see a full Earth.

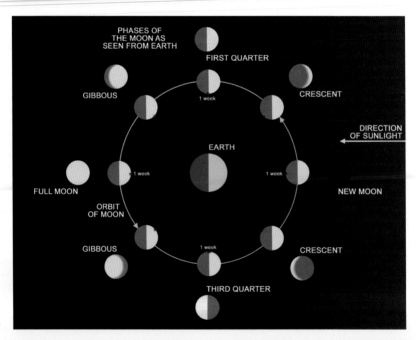

As this diagram demonstrates, half the Moon is always illuminated throughout its orbit (excluding lunar eclipses), even as humans observe full, gibbous, quarter, crescent, or new moons from Earth's surface.

If the climate of Earth kept changing drastically at frequent intervals, life would have a hard time keeping up. But by moderating Earth's wobble, the Moon helped create a relatively stable and temperate climate that helped contribute to the rapid evolution of life on our planet.

Tides created by the Moon may also have helped the earliest life-forms to appear on our planet. As tides recede from rocky shores, they can leave behind large puddles of still water, or tidal pools, which are quiet, shallow, and protected from predators. They may have offered shelter where the first living creatures could develop without facing the dangers of the open seas.

3

WORLDS OF ICE

Earth's moon is made of the same stuff Earth is: rock and metal. But a moon can be made of other things. A very common material found on moons is ordinary water ice, the same as might be found in a freezer. Some moons are made almost entirely of ice, while others are a mixture of rock and ice, like a dirty snowball, or a thick layer of ice over a rocky core. Many of the largest moons in the solar system are ice moons, and almost all of them belong to the four gas giant planets: Jupiter, Saturn, Uranus, and Neptune.

JUPITER'S ICE MOONS

Of Jupiter's four large moons, three are ice or mostly ice: Europa, Callisto, and Ganymede. Ice is also a key component of three very small moons that orbit much closer to Jupiter than the Galilean moons. These are the potato-shaped Metis, Adrastea, and Amalthea. The largest and most interesting, Amalthea, has an average diameter of

104 miles (167 km), and the smallest, Adrastea, is just 20 miles (32 km) wide. All three are made of ice or a mixture of ice and rock, are heavily cratered, and exhibit a vivid red color. Amalthea, in fact, is the reddest object in the solar system. Its color may be due to Io's volcanoes, which emit sulfur compounds that blow away and spiral toward Jupiter, coating the tiny inner moons. This red color is likely a relatively thin surface coating. At places, the underlying ice seems to peek through in white patches.

Water ice is not the only type of ice. Any frozen liquid or gas can be called an ice. For instance, dry ice is solid carbon dioxide gas. The polar caps of Mars and many comets consist of dry ice, while much of the surface of Pluto is ammonia ice.

Amalthea gives off more heat than it receives from the sun. Scientists are not sure how. The heat may be the result of tidal flexing—heat generated by the friction caused by gravity as the tiny moon orbits Jupiter. Or Jupiter's powerful magnetic field might create electrical currents within the moon that cause the heating.

A visitor to Amalthea would also notice that some of Amalthea's craters are very large in proportion to the size of the moon. One crater, Pan, is 60 miles (97 km) wide and 5 miles (8 km) deep, more than a third of the size of Amalthea. Another large crater, Gaea, is 50 miles (80 km) wide and possibly twice as deep as Pan. Both Metis and Adrastea look similar to Amalthea, pockmarked with craters.

These three small, irregular moons probably did not originate in their present positions. Billions of years ago, when Jupiter was forming, the planet was much too hot to allow icy bodies to form nearby. Metis, Adrastea, and Amalthea may have been comets that formed somewhere else in the solar system, wandered too close to Jupiter, and were captured by the giant planet's gravity.

CALLISTO

The surface of Callisto is a mix of rocks and ice, a mixture that may extend all the way to the moon's core. Scientists suspect there may be a warm, salty ocean buried about 155 miles (250 km) beneath the surface, mixed with a layer of rocks. The existence of this rocky layer is intriguing to astronomers because water interacting with the rocks might spur chemical reactions that could give rise to life. One piece of evidence pointing to the existence of this ocean is that Jupiter's magnetic field does not penetrate Callisto's surface. This implies a layer of electrically conductive fluid—perhaps water with salts and minerals dissolved in it—at least 6 miles (10 km) deep. This ocean puts Callisto on the list of possible sources of life in the solar system. Callisto even has a very thin atmosphere—a trillion times thinner than Earth's. The *Galileo* orbiter discovered that the atmosphere is mostly carbon dioxide,

THE GALILEAN MOONS

When Galileo Galilei turned his telescope toward Jupiter, he made a surprising discovery. "There were three starlets," he wrote on January 7, 1610, "small indeed, but very bright." Much to his surprise, when he looked at Jupiter again on the following night, the three little stars had moved! He realized that Jupiter's "stars" are actually satellites orbiting the planet. These satellites moved "about Jupiter as do Venus and Mercury about the sun," he wrote. Galileo had discovered not only that Jupiter is a world but also that it has moons. These four moons have been named the Galilean moons in honor of his discovery.

A VISIT TO CALLISTO

While Callisto has many craters, one enormous impact feature stands out among all the rest. The crater Valhalla is a series of concentric rings that resembles a bull's-eye some 1,500 miles (2,400 km) wide. Scarps surround the rings.

Seeing Callisto's thousands of craters wouldn't be the only reason to visit this moon. One especially strange feature might attract future space tourists: a region of jagged pinnacles of ice. These penitentes, or spires, can rise up to 45 feet (15 m) tall. These icy spikes formed through sublimation—when ice turns directly into water vapor without melting into a liquid first—which can occur in low pressure or high temperature environments. Irregularities in the surface cause the ice in some places to disappear faster than others, leaving behind an impressive collection of fang-like spires.

One of the most striking sights on Callisto, however, would be in the sky. From the surface of Callisto, Jupiter would appear more than eight times larger than a full moon in the night sky on Earth. Since Callisto, like the other Galilean moons, always keeps one face toward Jupiter, the planet would never rise or set.

Ice penitentes on Callisto

but a trace amount of oxygen has been found. Only three other moons in the solar system are known to have atmospheres.

Seen from space, Callisto is covered with thousands of craters. Its surface is about four billion years old—almost as old as the solar system. It has been pummeled endlessly by comets and asteroids, causing Callisto to be the most heavily cratered body in the solar system. No new crater can be created without overlapping an older one.

Scientists have found that the surface of Callisto is one of the oldest in the solar system. They discovered this by counting craters. The number of craters on the surface of a moon or planet reveals the age of that surface. Earth was once as heavily cratered as the Moon, but billions of years of renewal such as geologic activity and erosion have erased most of the ancient craters. The surface of Earth we are familiar with is much younger, geologically speaking, than the surface of the Moon, which has changed very little in the same time. Generally, astronomers assume that the more craters there are, the older the surface of an object is, while the presence of fewer craters indicates a younger surface. The large number of craters on Callisto tells scientists that its surface has changed very little since its formation.

Most of Callisto's craters don't look very much like those on Earth's moon. Instead, they are very flat and shallow. This tells scientists that the surface is made probably mostly of ice, which gradually flows like ice in a glacier. A crater on icy Callisto would eventually flatten out, like a hole scooped in mud.

GANYMEDE

Ganymede, the largest moon in the solar system, is bigger than the planet Mercury and one and a half times larger than our moon. It has a small iron core. Around this is a thick layer of rock and above that a layer of ice nearly 500 miles (800 km) thick.

One outstanding feature of many ice moons is their lack of outstanding features. Because ice is not as rigid as rock, it tends to

A VISIT TO GANYMEDE

Since Ganymede is closer to Jupiter than Callisto, Jupiter would seem even larger in the sky—nearly fifteen times larger than a full moon as seen from Earth. Surrounding any astronaut on Ganymede's surface would be a rolling landscape covered with craters and long, meandering grooves flanked by ridges as high as 2,000 feet (610 m). The grooves would stretch for thousands of miles in every direction.

slowly flow over time, as glaciers do on Earth. Tall mountains, deep craters, and canyons tend to flatten out. Indeed, one of the most noticeable features of Ganymede is its general flatness. However, crisscrossing the icy surface of the moon are dozens of long, curved cracks. Many of these cracks are surrounded by orange and brown hues, which might be organic material that spewed up through the crack from deep within the moon.

The surface of Ganymede looks very different from that of Callisto. While Ganymede also has large areas of heavy cratering, an equal amount of its surface is covered with complex patterns of grooves and ridges. These are probably formed when its icy crust shifts. Huge blocks of ice create long, meandering pressure ridges when they collide.

EUROPA

Europa is the sixth-largest moon in the solar system, making it only about 10 percent smaller than Earth's moon. If Europa replaced our moon, it would be about the same size in the sky, but because Europa is covered with ice instead of rock, it would appear more than five times brighter.

The surface of Europa is very smooth, with no prominent features such as deep craters and canyons or high mountains. This indicates that Europa's surface is very young compared to the age of the moon

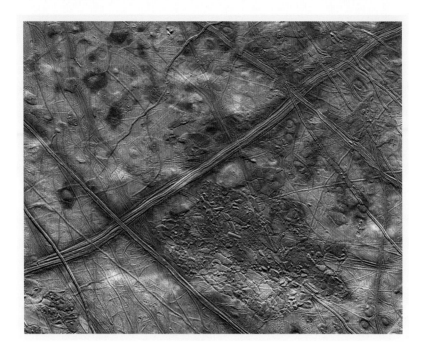

NASA scientists enhanced the colors on this photograph of Europa's surface. The bluer sections indicate relatively pure water ice, while the redder stripes probably contain various salts and would be good candidates for the landing site of a future probe.

itself. Some forces are at work that constantly renew the surface so that features are destroyed. The close resemblance of Europa's surface to the ice floes of the Arctic and Antarctic regions of Earth provides scientists with a clue as to what is happening. The visible surface of Europa is really just a thick layer of ice atop a deep ocean of liquid water. What observers see of Europa is the surface of a shell of ice 10 to 15 miles (15 to 25 km) thick. The ice floats on an ocean 40 to 100 miles (64 to 161 km) deep—a huge amount of water. Even though Europa is four times smaller than Earth, it contains twice as much water as all the oceans on Earth combined.

As the ice floating atop this ocean moves, it causes ridges, cracks, and grooves to form. Meanwhile, ice slowly erases craters and any other prominent features. Water squeezes up through the cracks and then freezes, creating a new, fresh surface. Geysers also eject water, spraying icy crystals that cover the surface in fresh ice.

A VISIT TO EUROPA

Europa, the smoothest body in the solar system, has no high mountains, deep valleys, or impressive craters. But there may be a few places worth a visit by future tourists. One might be a region of penitentes. The recent discovery of plumes of water vapor suggests that Europa may have active geysers too.

Europa's smooth, icy surface might be perfect for cross-country skiing—skiers would have to watch out for geysers, though!

FACTS ABOUT JUPITER'S LARGE ICE MOONS

Name	Diameter	Distance from Jupiter	Time to orbit Jupiter
Ganymede	3,270 miles (5,262 km)	665,000 miles (1.07 million km)	7.155 days
Callisto	2,995 miles (4,820 km)	1.17 million miles (1.88 million km)	16.689 days
Europa	1,940 miles (3,122 km)	417,000 miles (671,000 km)	3.551 days

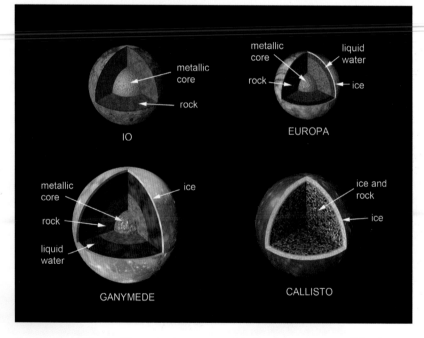

This diagram exhibits the different interior structures of the four Galilean moons. Io differs from the other three, as it doesn't show signs of subsurface ice or liquid water. Europa's subsurface ocean has been of great interest to astronomers in the search for extraterrestrial life.

OTHER ICY WORLDS

Many of the larger moons of Saturn—including Mimas, Tethys, Dione, Rhea, and Iapetus—are made mostly of ice. Uranus too has several icy moons, such as Miranda and Umbriel. They all have small rocky cores or are a mix of ice and rock.

Especially interesting to astronomers is Enceladus, a moon of Saturn. It is only about 314 miles (505 km) in diameter, but this small moon has a big secret: a sea of warm, liquid water buried deep beneath its icy crust. Scientists first suspected the existence of the ocean when they discovered enormous geysers of salty water erupting from cracks in Enceladus's southern hemisphere. This ocean is the subject of much research as astronomers search for life on other worlds.

Like Jupiter's ice moons, Neptune's largest moon, Triton, also has a rocky core covered with frozen nitrogen. However, that icy coating is much thinner than that of any of Jupiter's moons. Triton's surface consists mostly of smooth, flat plains with only a few scattered craters. Seen from space, large regions of small, low, rolling hills make much of Triton resemble the surface of a cantaloupe.

Even bodies orbiting at the very frontiers of the solar system have moons. The dwarf planet Pluto has a large moon named Charon. Although Pluto is very small—only 1,473 miles (2,370 km) wide—Charon is half the size of Pluto at 753 miles (1,212 km) wide, making it the largest moon in the solar system compared to the body it orbits. Charon was discovered entirely by accident in 1978 when astronomers examining a photo of Pluto noticed a strange lump on one side of the dwarf planet. The lump was a large moon that was just coming into view as it circled Pluto.

Like similar icy worlds, Charon probably has a small rocky core. But otherwise it is made entirely of ice, with a surface covered in frozen water, ammonia, and nitrogen. Charon is mostly grayish, with patches of faint oranges and browns. These are probably from gases—nitrogen, carbon monoxide, and methane—that escaped from Pluto's atmosphere.

Enceladus's watery plumes would be a
fantastic sight for any explorer.

An illustration of Pluto as seen from Charon's Argo Chasma

Solar radiation causes these gases to react with Charon's composition to form reddish compounds of organic molecules (molecules that contain carbon and hydrogen). Like Europa and Enceladus, Charon may have cryogeysers—geysers that spread fresh ices over its surface.

One of Charon's most distinguishing features is a "super Grand Canyon" called Argo Chasma. It is nearly 430 miles (692 km) long. By comparison, Earth's Grand Canyon in Arizona is only 277 miles (446 km) long. Argo Chasma may be as deep as 5.5 miles (9 km), more than five times the depth of the Grand Canyon. Charon may also have sheer, vertical cliffs several miles high, rivaling Verona Rupes on Uranus's moon Miranda.

Pluto's four other moons are very small. The two largest are only about 25 miles (40 km) wide. They are all coated with a thick layer of almost pure water ice. Scientists believe that all of Pluto's moons, including Charon, might be the result of a collision between Pluto and another object, an origin similar to that of Earth's moon.

4

A WORLD
OF FIRE

Perhaps the most unusual moon in the solar system is Jupiter's Io. At first glance, Io resembles a cheese pizza, with its blotchy, swirling patterns of red, yellow, orange, and white. It is a large moon, about 2 percent bigger than our own. Unlike Jupiter's other giant moons, Io seems to have little or no ice.

Io is the most volcanic body in the solar system. Its surface has no impact craters but, instead, it has hundreds of volcanic calderas, or large flat-floored craters. Many are violently active. Io has more than 400 volcanoes, and at least 150 of them are active at any one time—far more than on Earth.

Some of the most powerful of Io's volcanic eruptions can throw bright plumes of material as high as 186 miles (300 km) above the surface. But these eruptions look nothing like those we see on our planet. Since Io has very little atmosphere, the dust and gas cannot create the billowing clouds we see spewing from volcanoes on Earth.

The dark spots scattered across Io's surface are sites of recent volcanic activity. The *Galileo* spacecraft saw one such area appear and erupt over the course of its mission.

Instead, Io's volcanoes look like huge garden sprinklers, the gas and dust curving in enormous arcs, forming umbrella-shaped plumes over the vents.

Tidal flexing caused by Jupiter creates Io's internal heat. The tides generated by two other larger, nearby moons—Europa and Callisto—also affect this heat. The combination of these forces causes the surface of Io to rise and fall by as much as 300 feet (91 m) in the forty-three hours it takes the moon to make a single orbit of Jupiter. This movement creates a huge amount of friction within the crust of the moon, and this generates vast amounts of heat that power Io's volcanoes.

TUG-OF-WAR

The force of gravity decreases with distance. As a moon orbits a planet, the planet's gravity pulls primarily on the side of the moon that is closest to it and less forcefully on the side that is farther away. The uneven pull is a tidal force. On Earth the tidal force of the Moon's gravity results in the regular rise and fall of the oceans.

Tidal forces can cause a moon to flex like a rubber ball being repeatedly squeezed in your fist. If the flexing is strong enough, it can generate great amounts of heat. To see how this works for yourself, bend a paper clip back and forth until it breaks, and then feel the ends of the broken pieces. They will feel warm. In the same way, the flexing of a moon by tidal forces will cause it to heat up.

Tidal flexing is the source of the heat that powers Io's volcanoes and keeps the subsurface water oceans of other moons, such as Europa and Enceladus, warm and liquid.

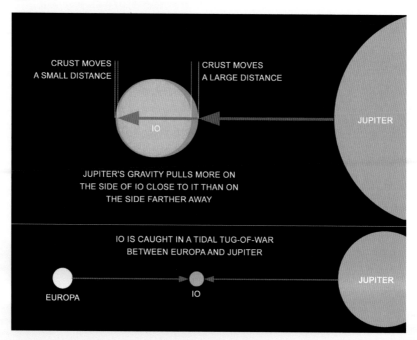

This diagram illustrates the process of tidal flexing as it affects Io.

Since Io is much smaller than Earth, its gravity is weaker. Some of the material that its volcanoes throw into the sky leaves the moon altogether. This forms a thin cloud that extends all the way around Io's orbit.

Some of Io's volcanoes spew molten rock, like volcanoes on Earth, while others erupt molten sulfur compounds. Because sulfur's color is temperature-dependent, the sulfur gives Io its extraordinary hues. Scientists find it almost impossible to chart a map of Io, as about 0.004 inches (0.01 cm) of new material is constantly flowing onto the surface each year. About half a mile (0.8 km) is added to the surface of Io every one hundred thousand years.

REMARKABLE MOUNTAINS

Oddly enough, almost none of Io's mountains are volcanoes. But they probably came from Io's intense volcanic activity.

Unlike most of Earth's mountains—such as the Rocky Mountains, the Andes, or the Alps—Io's aren't in chains or groups. They sit alone and isolated on Io's volcanic plains. Some of them are ragged ridges or tilted, sharp-edged blocks, while others resemble the flat-topped mesas of the American Southwest.

One of Io's mountains, Euboea Montes, is 6.8 miles (11 km) high, or 1.4 miles (2.2 km) taller than Mount Everest. Another mountain, Tohil Mons, is far from Io's tallest mountain at 18,000 feet (5,400 m), but it might be one of the most impressive. Resembling Switzerland's Matterhorn, it towers like a monument above the nearly flat landscape of volcanic pits and lakes of molten sulfur that surrounds it.

Astronomers think that these mountains might be the result of all the new material that the erupting volcanoes constantly add to the surface. The weight of the new material presses down on the surface crust, cracking it into large blocks. As one part of a block is forced down, another part will be forced up, similar to what occurs when you press down on one end of a piece of floating wood. As one end of the block sinks, the other rises, creating mountains.

A VISIT TO IO

If humans could find a way to resist the intense radiation that exists close to Jupiter, the surface of Io would be a memorable place to visit. There are deep calderas filled with lakes of boiling sulfur, steaming fumaroles, and huge flat-topped mountains slowly melting into the surrounding surface like giant pats of butter. The landscape is covered with a thick blanket of colorful sulfur compounds that either flow from the volcanic vents or are deposited from the eruptions.

The volcanoes aren't the cone-shaped mountains we are used to seeing on Earth—such as Mount Vesuvius or Mount Saint Helens—but instead are calderas filled with molten rock and sulfur. When they erupt, they throw fountains of molten material high into the dark sky. Visitors would have to be careful, watching out not only for the eruptions but also for rocky debris falling back to the ground.

The volcanoes would not be the only remarkable sight. Since Io orbits just 262,000 miles (421,648 km) from Jupiter—closer than our moon is from Earth—the giant planet Jupiter fills Io's sky like an enormous striped balloon, forty times larger than a full moon in Earth's sky. Because Io, like our moon, keeps one side always facing its planet, Jupiter never rises or sets but always stays in the same place in the sky.

During Io's day, the sun will pass behind the planet. For a few hours Jupiter will look like a huge dark hole in the sky, rimmed all the way around by a red ring as sunlight passes through the giant planet's atmosphere. A visitor might be able to see bright flashes of lightning on the dark side of Jupiter, while yellowish auroras dance in the sky. Radiation from Jupiter creates these auroras, causing gases high in Io's tenuous atmosphere to glow, much as the electricity flowing through the glass tube of a neon light causes the gas inside the tube to glow.

VOLCANOES!

In 1979 scientist Linda Morabito was examining one of the latest photos of Io sent back by the *Voyager 1* spacecraft. She noticed something strange in the picture. There appeared to be a large crescent-shaped cloud extending past the edge of the moon. But since Io has no atmosphere, it couldn't be a cloud. It could only be a huge, ongoing volcanic eruption. The next day, *Voyager 1* found several other volcanic plumes. These were the first active volcanoes to be discovered on a world other than Earth.

A volcanic eruption on Io, with the distant sun and Europa visible in the sky

ICE VOLCANOES AND ICE GEYSERS

While Io is the only moon in the solar system with volcanoes powered by molten rock and sulfur, two other moons have volcano-like features powered by hot water and ice. Because these volcanoes erupt ice rather than molten rock, astronomers call them cryovolcanoes or cryogeysers, where *cryo* means "cold." Despite being cold, cryovolcanoes and cryogeysers are probably powered by heat generated deep within the moon by tidal flexing.

Scientists suspect Jupiter's Europa has cryogeysers because they've detected water vapor being ejected from its surface. But the most impressive cryogeysers are found on Enceladus, a moon of Saturn. In 2005 the *Cassini* spacecraft discovered giant cryogeysers erupting from Enceladus's surface near its south pole. These geysers are very powerful. Vast, feathery plumes of water vapor and ice particles leave the vents at jet engine speed, shooting as far as 124 miles (200 km) above the surface. To see one close up would be like looking at a huge rocket engine.

Neptune's giant moon Triton has its own unique cryovolcanoes. The eruptions create dark plumes that rise as high as 5 miles (8 km) into the sky. These volcanoes do not erupt molten rock like volcanoes on Earth, molten sulfur like those on Io, or water ice like Enceladus's geysers. Instead, they erupt liquid nitrogen, methane, and dust.

Triton has a very thin atmosphere. The surface pressure is only about one seven-thousandth that of Earth's atmosphere. Made up mostly of nitrogen, it extends 500 miles (800 km) above the surface. Even though Triton's atmosphere is very thin—its surface pressure is only 0.000015 times that of Earth—it is still dense enough to support a high-altitude layer of haze, clouds, and strong winds. These winds give Triton's geysers a very peculiar appearance. Their plumes shoot straight up for miles until they reach the level where the wind is blowing. Then the plume goes off at a right angle, like a flag in a breeze.

NASA's proposed *Trident* mission would travel to Triton to attempt to understand what drives the moon's geysers.

5

THE GIANT

S aturn's largest moon, Titan, is one of the strangest places in the
solar system. One of the largest moons in the solar system, at
3,200 miles (5,150 km) in diameter, it's about 50 percent bigger
than Earth's moon. Titan has a very dense atmosphere filled with thick
clouds that cover the moon from pole to pole. Through a telescope,
Titan looks like an orange tennis ball.

Until recently, no one had any idea what the surface of Titan might
look like or what might be there. Radar from Earth, bounced off the
surface of Titan, gave vague hints of geological features, but no one
could tell what they were. In 2004 the *Cassini* orbiter arrived at Saturn,
and some of the mysteries surrounding Titan began to be unveiled.

Because *Cassini* was so close to Titan, its radar was able to resolve
much finer details than any Earth-based radar could. The very first
images revealed a surprising variety of geologic features, including
a few impact craters as well as channels, cryovolcanic features, and
wind-blown deposits that looked like dunes. As the orbiter continued
its mapping, even more surprising features showed up, including what
looked like lakes and rivers. The radar images also revealed that Titan

Cassini photographed Ligeia Mare, a methane and ethane lake on Titan, several times during its mission. In 2013 and 2014, it observed a strange feature near the lake's edge about 12.5 miles (20 km) long that has since disappeared. Scientists do not know if it was an island, an iceberg, or something else.

had very few craters, and those that it had were very eroded—a sign that Titan had rain and wind wearing away at the rock. The seas were hundreds of miles wide, hundreds of feet deep, and so clear that the radar could see their bottoms.

Eventually, scientists created a detailed map of the entire moon using the data from *Cassini*'s radar.

As the *Cassini* orbiter flew past Titan in 2005, it released the *Huygens* probe. The probe parachuted into Titan's atmosphere and made a safe landing on the surface. On the way down, it took dozens

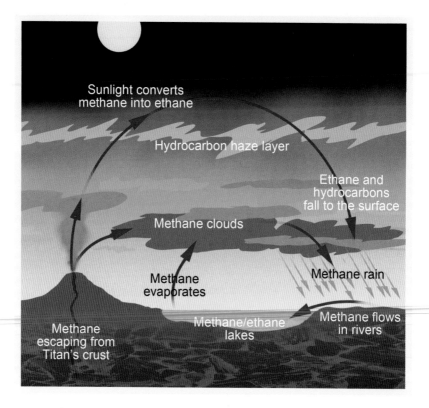

Titan's methane cycle is an analog to Earth's water cycle. The sun causes surface liquid methane to evaporate into Titan's atmosphere. Scientists have also begun to study how the methane cycle on Titan changes with the moon's seasons.

of photos of the landscape beneath it. The probe's batteries lasted for only 153 minutes, including 72 minutes on the surface of Titan. But during that short time, the *Huygens* returned much valuable data to the scientists waiting back on Earth, including information about the composition, density, temperature, and pressure of Titan's atmosphere.

The *Huygens* photos revealed scenery that looked very much like Earth, with hills and river channels and shorelines. But there was a critical difference: Titan's lakes and rivers are made of methane, not water. Methane is a poisonous, flammable gas. It's the main component of natural gas that humans use for heat and cooking. On Earth, methane composes only about 0.00017 percent of the atmosphere. On Titan it composes 5 percent. The rest of Titan's atmosphere is nitrogen. There is little or no oxygen, so it would be impossible for a human to breathe there.

Titan is very cold. Its surface is a frigid –290°F (–179°C). By comparison, dry ice, or frozen carbon dioxide, is only –109°F (–79°C). At these temperatures, water freezes to ice as hard as steel, but methane gas becomes a liquid. Whereas our planet has a water cycle, Titan has a methane cycle. As the seasons on Titan slowly change, storm clouds made of methane form low above the moon's surface. These clouds produce downpours of methane rain. The methane flows in streams and rivers, filling vast lakes and seas, before slowly evaporating back into the atmosphere. Some of this methane also soaks into the ground, where it is eventually released into the atmosphere by cryogeysers and cryovolcanoes.

TITAN'S ATMOSPHERE

Titan is the only moon in the solar system known to have a substantial atmosphere. Because Titan's gravity is much weaker than that on Earth, the atmosphere extends nearly ten times higher than it does on our planet, about 370 miles (600 km) above the surface and produces a surface pressure much greater than what we experience on our planet. If you were to visit the surface of Titan, you would feel the same pressure on your body as you would if you were swimming about 50 feet (15 m) underwater.

Not all the methane released from the volcanoes or evaporated from the seas winds up in the cycle. Some of it rises much higher into the atmosphere of Titan, high enough for the sun's ultraviolet energy to split apart the methane and nitrogen molecules. These fragments then recombine to form a large variety of organic molecules. Some of these molecules sift down through the atmosphere in the form of a dark dust or grains. Others create a kind of smog—the thick, orange haze that blankets Titan from pole to pole and hides its surface from Earth-bound telescopes.

A VISIT TO TITAN

If you were to visit Titan, the landscapes you would see would be very familiar in some ways. There are hills, mountains, sand dunes, rivers, streams, and lakes. The scenery is sculpted by erosion, just as on Earth, except this erosion is caused by liquid methane instead of water. Much of the surface is covered with the brown and orange organic molecules that constantly drift down from the upper atmosphere.

Much of Titan's equatorial region is covered in hundreds of square miles of dunes that look very much like those in the Sahara on Earth. Instead of sand, though, these dunes are made up of dark hydrocarbon grains that scientists think would resemble coffee grounds up close.

Unlike on the Moon or Mars, there are very few impact craters. As has happened on Earth, Titan's impact craters have been largely erased by flowing liquid, wind erosion, and tectonic forces—the movement of the moon's crust, volcanoes, and earthquakes. Besides volcanoes, Titan has mountains, most ranging from only about 3,280 feet to 5,000 feet (1,000 m to 1,524 m) tall. One mountain range in the southern hemisphere stretches for 93 miles (150 km). The mountains are mostly water ice covered in methane snow. One reason that Titan's mountains don't get very high is because water ice is not as strong as rock. If a mountain gets too big, it will begin to flow, like a glacier on Earth.

Scattered across the landscape are many lakes and seas. To a visitor, these would look very similar to bodies of water on Earth. You might even see icebergs floating in the distance. Flowing into these lakes are many meandering rivers and streams.

Scientists at the California Institute of Technology modeled Titan's rainfall. They found that the area around Titan's equator can sometimes go for years without any rain at all. But when rain does occur, the storms are heavy enough to carve out the channels that *Huygens* observed on Titan's surface.

A vast underground ocean of liquid water runs deep beneath the surface of Titan. Lying 35 to 50 miles (55 to 80 km) underground, the water in this ocean is mixed with ammonia and salts. This body of water makes Titan a member of a very exclusive club. Only four other worlds in the solar system are known to possess large underground reservoirs of water: Jupiter's Europa and Ganymede, Saturn's Enceladus, and the dwarf planet Pluto (though scientists suspect oceans may lie beneath Callisto and other moons as well). Because these oceans are warm and their waters are filled with molecules and chemicals that are the building blocks of life, scientists are very interested in searching for life in these places. The seas and lakes on Titan might even harbor some form of life.

A COSMIC GAS STATION

In the future, Titan may become akin to a gas station in orbit around Saturn, where a spacecraft could refuel for a trip back to Earth or even farther out into the solar system—to Uranus, Neptune, Pluto, or beyond. Methane is a highly flammable gas. Compressed into a liquid and pumped into a spacecraft's tanks, it makes an excellent rocket fuel. To burn it, astronauts would merely have to add oxygen, which the spacecraft could either carry from Earth or obtain from the ice in Saturn's rings or one of its small moons.

A storm stirs up waves in one of Titan's frigid methane seas.

One thing a visitor to Titan probably will *not* see is Saturn. While Jupiter dominates the skies of its moons, a few of Titan's skies would show only clouds, stretching from horizon to horizon. If Saturn were to ever be visible—which scientists think almost never happens—it would appear ten times larger than a full moon on Earth.

A GLIMPSE INTO THE PAST

Except for the extreme cold, Titan is very similar to early Earth. Earth's first atmosphere was composed mainly of gases that came from volcanoes. These included hydrogen sulfide, methane, and from ten to two hundred times more carbon dioxide than is in the atmosphere today. Up to 2.5 billion years ago, methane droplets in the air shrouded young Earth in a global haze, just like the one that blankets Titan. Oxygen did not exist on its own and occurred only in compounds such as water.

Three billion years ago, the sun was only about 70 percent as bright as it is today. Earth would have been frozen if not for the greenhouse gases in the atmosphere. These gases—mainly methane and carbon dioxide—trapped enough of the sun's heat to keep the planet from freezing. A similar process occurs on Titan. Greenhouse gases—also mainly methane—in its atmosphere keep its surface an average of 22°F (12°C) warmer than it would be otherwise. Titan's surface is still very, very cold, though—much colder than Earth has ever been.

Studying Titan is in many ways like traveling back to visit Earth billions of years ago, when the first life-forms appeared. The first living organisms on Earth didn't need oxygen. Instead, they obtained energy from sulfur and other elements. The same thing may be happening on Titan, deep within the warm underground seas or around the cryothermal features many scientists believe exist on its surface, such as hot springs and geysers.

6

THE PLANET WITH A BILLION MOONS

Nothing in the solar system is quite like Saturn's rings. Jupiter, Uranus, and Neptune all have ring systems, but these are composed largely of dust, so they are dark, thin, and invisible to even the most powerful Earth-based telescopes. But Saturn's rings are very bright—for instance, the broad middle ring, also known as the B ring, reflects more sunlight than Saturn itself.

Unlike the rings of the other planets, which are mostly made of dark dust, Saturn's rings are made of billions of individual chunks of

Each chunk of ice and rock that comprises Saturn's rings may be considered an individual moon.

nearly pure water ice, much like the ice cubes in a bag at a convenience store. Most of the chunks are small, from a few millimeters to several feet. A few objects a half-mile (0.8 km) wide may also exist. If all the material in the rings could be compressed into a ball, it would form a moon only 60 miles (100 km) across. Some scientists think the rings may have once been an icy moon that never fully formed or a moon that was broken up by Saturn's gravity when its orbit carried it too close to the planet.

Planetary scientist Robin Canup recently proposed a theory about the origin of Saturn's rings. She suggests that a few hundred million years ago—when the early ancestors of the dinosaurs were roaming Earth—Saturn may have had no rings at all. According to her theory, the rings formed when one or more small moons wandered too close to Saturn. Tidal forces created by Saturn's gravity pulled the theorized moons apart. After millions of years of bumping against one another, the pieces of the destroyed objects were ground into the tiny particles that form the present-day rings.

Each of these particles is, in a sense, an individual moon, circling Saturn in its own orbit, making Saturn a planet with a billion moons.

TOO CLOSE FOR COMFORT

A planet exerts a gravitational pull on any moon that orbits it. The side of a moon that is closer to the planet gets attracted a little more than the opposite side, which is farther away. The closer a moon gets to the planet, the greater the difference between the pull on the closer side and the pull on the farther side. If a moon gets too close to its planet, the difference in gravitational pull can be great enough to tear the moon apart. The minimum distance at which a moon can orbit a planet without getting torn apart is called the Roche limit. Any material that might be orbiting within the Roche limit of a planet will never be able to form a moon. All the tiny moonlets that form Saturn's rings orbit within Saturn's Roche limit, which suggests that the rings are either the remains of a moon that strayed too close and was broken up or are material left over from the birth of Saturn that was unable to form a moon.

LORD OF THE RINGS

Many scientists think that Saturn's rings are relatively young. To determine the age of the rings, they look at how "clean" the ring particles are. Over time, particles of ice floating in the solar system gather a coating of dark dust, but Saturn's rings are still very bright and lack this distinctive coating. Scientists also look at the gravitational effects of all of Saturn's moons and have predicted that over many millions of years, these effects will make the rings unstable. The rings only look the way they do because the moons haven't had enough time to fully disrupt them. In a few million years, however, the rings will start to fall in toward Saturn, and the solar system will lose one of its greatest natural wonders.

The rings are unbelievably vast. They cover an area of over 15 billion square miles (40 billion sq. km), eighty times the total surface area of Earth. To travel from the inner edge of the rings to the outer edge, an astronaut would have to cover a distance equal to thirteen trips

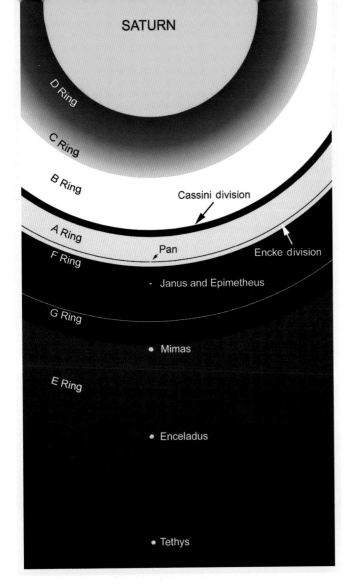

SATURN

D Ring

C Ring

B Ring

Cassini division

A Ring

F Ring

Pan

Encke division

Janus and Epimetheus

G Ring

• Mimas

E Ring

• Enceladus

• Tethys

The most distinctly visible rings of Saturn are the A, B, and C rings. Scientists have since discovered several other rings. The broad, hazy outermost ring, the E ring, is made primarily of microscopic particles that scientists believe come from Enceladus's geyser jets.

across the United States. They are so wide—175,000 miles (282,000 km) from inner to outer edge—that they would just barely fit between Earth and the Moon. The thickness of the rings, however, rarely exceeds 3,200 feet (975 m). The rings are so thin relative to their width that a sheet of writing paper 7 miles (11 km) wide would be proportionally as thick. If you were to condense the rings to just 3 feet (1 m) wide, they would be ten thousand times thinner than a razor blade.

WHY DO SATURN'S RINGS LOOK SOLID?

Any photograph printed in a newspaper looks like continuous tones of gray, but when you look at it closely, you can see the photograph is really made up of thousands of individual dots. It's the same for Saturn's rings. The individual particles orbiting Saturn are too small to be seen from a distance. Instead, they blend together just like the dots in a newspaper photo, giving the appearance of a solid ring.

The rings include three main bands, distinct enough to be visible through even small telescopes on Earth: the A, B, and C rings. The A ring and the broader, brighter B ring are separated by a space called the Cassini division. Despite the narrow appearance of the Cassini division, Earth's moon could actually fit inside it! Inside the B ring is the dim, translucent C ring, also called the crepe ring because of its relatively dark color.

These main bands are not the only rings around Saturn. Even before the advent of spacecraft, astronomers were aware of at least the very narrow outer F ring. The *Pioneer* and *Voyager* probes discovered many more. And *Voyager* found that the A and B rings were made up of five hundred to one thousand extremely narrow rings, like the grooves on a phonograph record. Many of these subrings are created or maintained by "shepherd moons," tiny moonlets that orbit Saturn within the gaps between rings. Although these little moons are less than 30 miles (46 km) wide, they are still larger than the particles that make up the rings. As they circle Saturn within its rings, they leave wakes and create waves, like a boat traveling up a river. These effects help keep the gaps in the rings clear of ice particles.

7

PRISONERS OF GRAVITY

Floating around the solar system are rocky bodies, or asteroids, ranging from only a few feet to many miles wide. Most asteroids orbit the sun in the asteroid belt, a region between Mars and Jupiter. The largest asteroid, Ceres, at 300 miles (483 km) wide, is big enough that astronomers consider it a dwarf planet.

Early on in the solar system's formation, when the planets were still very young, asteroids were flying around everywhere. Many collided with the planets and their moons, creating huge craters that are still visible. Not even Earth was spared from bombardment, but weather and geologic forces over millions of years have erased all but a few of our planet's ancient craters.

Not all of these wayward asteroids collided with planets. A few were captured by planets' gravity in such a way that they went into orbit as satellites. Among the moons that astronomers suspect were originally asteroids are the two moons of Mars, Phobos and Deimos.

Millions of years in the future Phobos (*above*) may approach too close to Mars and be broken up, while Deimos (*right*, as photographed by the *Mars Reconnaissance Orbiter*) will escape orbit.

One clue scientists have is the moons' appearance: they are lumpy and potato-shaped, like asteroids, rather than spherical. They are also among the smallest moons in the solar system. Phobos is only 14 miles (22 km) wide, while Deimos is only 8 miles (13 km) across.

Phobos, which orbits Mars more closely than Deimos does, is creeping a few fractions of an inch closer to the planet every year. In the next forty or fifty million years, it will pass within Mars's Roche limit and be destroyed. After Mars's gravity pulls it apart, Phobos might become a ring around Mars similar to those of Saturn. Deimos, Mars's outer moon, is moving farther and farther away from Mars. Eventually it will escape into space.

IRREGULAR MOONS

Of the more than two hundred moons in the solar system, more than half may be captured asteroids or comets. This includes more than seventy of Jupiter's nearly eighty moons. Most of Jupiter's captured moons are very small. The most recently discovered one, Valetudo, is only about half a mile (1 km) wide. Saturn has thirty-eight of these tiny moons, and Uranus has at least nine.

Two types of moon are in the solar system: regular and irregular. Regular moons are large satellites with nearly circular orbits in the same plane as the planet's equator. Regular moons also orbit in the same direction as the planet's rotation. Earth's moon, Europa, and Titan are regular moons. Irregular moons are usually very small, with orbits that are much more elliptical and much more tilted relative to the

SOME ARE ROUND, AND SOME ARE NOT

Why are some bodies in the solar system round like balls and others lumpy and potato-like? The answer has to do with gravity. A planet's gravity pulls equally from all sides. If an object—such as Earth—is big enough, this pull is stronger than the material it is made of. So gravity, pulling from every direction, shapes the object into a sphere. But if the object is small enough, the rock and metal it is made of might be too strong for its gravity to overcome. So it can be pretty much any shape. For a moon made mostly of rock, like Earth's moon, the minimum diameter required to become a sphere is about 373 miles (600 km). For one made mostly of water ice, such as Europa, the minimum size is 249 miles (400 km). For anything smaller than this, the moon's gravity won't overcome the strength of the object's material, causing it to take on a lumpy shape, such as Mars's moons.

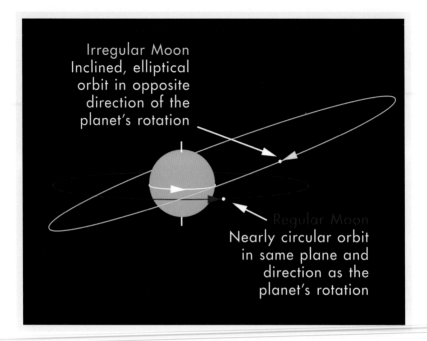

Irregular Moon
Inclined, elliptical
orbit in opposite
direction of the
planet's rotation

Regular Moon
Nearly circular orbit
in same plane and
direction as the
planet's rotation

The degree to which an object's orbit is skewed from a perfect circle is called the eccentricity of the orbit. The more eccentric the orbit, the more extreme the ellipse. The highly eccentric orbits of irregular moons are a key indicator that the moons were captured.

planet's equator. They even sometimes orbit their planet in the opposite direction of the planet's rotation.

The largest irregular moon in the solar system is Neptune's Triton. At 1,680 miles (2,700 km) across, it's larger than Pluto and the seventh-largest moon in the solar system. It even resembles Pluto in size and composition. Although Triton's orbit is nearly circular, it is in the opposite direction of Neptune's spin. To astronomers that's a sure giveaway that a moon was captured. The orbit is also tipped at a steep angle relative to the planet's rotation. The rest of Neptune's moons are tiny, rocky satellites. The largest, Proteus, is only 260 miles (420 km) wide. Neptune's third-largest moon, Nereid, has one of the most eccentric orbits of any moon in the solar system. It was probably originally a regular moon, and when Neptune captured Triton, its orbit was displaced due to gravitational effects.

HOW MANY MOONS DOES EARTH HAVE?

Is the Moon the only moon Earth has? The Moon is the only permanent natural satellite of Earth, but our planet regularly gains and loses many temporary moons. Every so often, a small asteroid—usually only a few feet wide—will go into a short-lived orbit around Earth before eventually burning up in the atmosphere or flying off into space again. The first such mini-moon ever observed was a tiny asteroid named 2006 RH120 after the year of its discovery. Less than a year later, though, it was gone. Scientists believe that Earth always has at least one temporary extra moon, typically only about 3 feet (1 m) in size. After being captured by Earth's gravity, the object will orbit about three times over the following ten months before being flung back off into space.

On February 15, 2020, astronomers Theodore Pruyne and Kacper Wierzchos found yet another mini-moon orbiting Earth. Designated 2020 CD3, it was little more than a large rock between 6.2 and 11.5 feet (1.9 and 3.5 m) wide. Pruyne and Wierzchos believe the mini-moon had been orbiting Earth for more than a year before they spotted it. Gravitational nudges from Earth, the Moon, and even the sun sent it back into space in March 2020.

Earth's mini-moons are too small to view with the naked eye. However, Earth has plenty of artificial satellites that you can see on a clear night.

REFRIGERATOR WORLD

The temperature at the surface of Triton is −391°F (−235°C). The methane, nitrogen, and carbon dioxide on Triton freeze solid and cover the ground in ice and frost, making the surface very bright. Triton's brightness is one reason that it is so cold: it reflects most of the heat it gets from the sun.

Triton may have originated from the Kuiper Belt, named after Gerard Kuiper, a Dutch astronomer. In 1951 Kuiper suggested that the solar system might be surrounded by a vast belt of icy bodies that stretched between thirty and fifty times farther away from the sun than Earth. These icy bodies—as many as two hundred million of them ranging from less than 6 miles (10 km) to over 1,100 miles (1,770 km) across—are the main source of the comets that occasionally sweep though the solar system. While most of the bodies in the Kuiper Belt are fairly small, a few of them are quite large—as large as Triton and Pluto. Could Triton, some astronomers wondered, be an object that strayed from the Kuiper Belt only to be captured by Neptune's gravity? One clue that suggests this possibility is Triton's composition, which closely resembles the typical icy Kuiper Belt body.

Scientist Thomas B. McCord in 1966 suggested the most generally accepted theory about the origin of Triton. Millions of years ago, Triton may have been a dwarf planet in its own orbit around the sun, but this orbit was a very eccentric one. Its distance from the sun varied greatly during the course of its long year. At some points in its orbit, it may have been as far away as Pluto, and sometimes it came inside the orbit of Neptune. Most of the time Triton's orbit passed above or below that of Neptune, like two highways crossing at an overpass. But just once, Neptune's and Triton's orbits crossed on the same plane, and the giant planet captured the smaller one.

8

CURIOUSER AND CURIOUSER

Some moons of the solar system are interesting to scientists mainly because they are so strange. They may be mysterious in origin, have some unique feature or odd behavior, or may look strange. Some moons are among the most unusual objects in the solar system.

MIRANDA

Uranus has five large moons. The innermost, Miranda, is just 293 miles (472 km) in diameter. Uranus is only 80,782 miles (130,000 km) away. From that distance, the planet would appear forty-four times larger than a full moon here on Earth and would nearly fill Miranda's sky.

Miranda is a very distinctive-looking moon. It appears to have been broken into pieces and imperfectly glued back together. The landscape is an uneven collection of valleys, cracks, grooves, and steep cliffs.

What caused Miranda to look so strange? Astronomers think that in the distant past, Miranda had a very different orbit than it does now. Sometimes the orbit brought it very close to Uranus, and sometimes the orbit took it far away. These drastic changes in gravity put a lot of stress on the little moon. The fluctuations in gravity caused ice deep within Miranda to melt. The circulation of this warmed material was probably

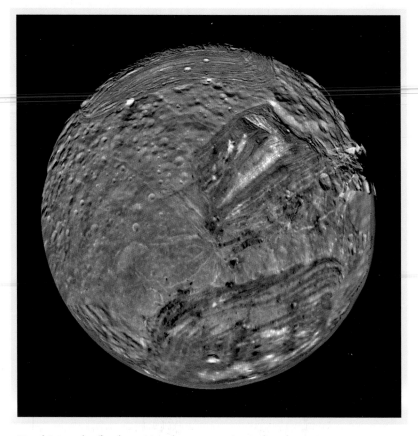

Miranda's jagged surface has captivated astronomers since its first observation.

what caused all of the fractures in Miranda's surface. Miranda's orbit has since become much more circular, with fewer stresses to warp the moon. Gravitational effects probably no longer heat the moon from the inside, and Miranda has frozen solid all the way through.

Something else may have contributed to Miranda's appearance. A giant planet such as Uranus attracts a great many comets and asteroids. Since Miranda is so close to Uranus, it is in more jeopardy of running into one of these stray objects than an outer moon would be. Possibly one of these asteroids was large enough to literally shatter Miranda into pieces, like a baseball hitting a glass fishbowl. The pieces remained in orbit around Uranus, where they eventually reassembled. Some astronomers suggest that this may have happened as often as five times to Miranda.

Whatever the causes may be, the landscape of tiny Miranda is one of the weirdest in the solar system. There are huge canyons as deep as 12 miles (20 km); winding, parallel ridges and valleys; and several steep, high scarps.

Verona Rupes—also known as the Great Wall of Miranda—is one of these scarps. It is a smooth wall nearly 3 miles (5 km) high, making it the tallest cliff in the solar system. By comparison, the Grand Canyon on Earth in only 1 mile (1.6 km) deep. Verona Rupes is also very steep, with a slope of about 45 degrees. The cliff was created when two vast blocks of Miranda's crust moved—one up and the other down. The great height of the cliff combined with the low gravity on Miranda would mean that a clumsy astronaut falling from the edge would take more than five minutes to reach the bottom. Even with Miranda's low gravity, the fall is so long that the astronaut would land at a speed of 124 miles (200 km) per hour.

IAPETUS

Long before anyone saw a close-up photo of Iapetus, Saturn's third-largest moon, astronomers knew there was something strange

An illustration of astronauts exploring Verona Rupes, the Great Wall of Miranda

about it. For one thing, its brightness changes as it orbits Saturn. It seems twice as bright during half of its orbit as it does during the other half. The only explanation scientists could think of was that half of Iapetus was almost black and the other half almost white. When the dark side is facing Earth, Iapetus looks dim. When the light side is facing Earth, Iapetus looks bright.

The first photos of Iapetus taken by the spacecraft *Voyager 2* in 1981 revealed that Iapetus is indeed nearly half black and half white, with a sharp, S-shaped dividing line between the two halves. The little moon looks a lot like the Chinese black-and-white yin-yang symbol. Scientists aren't certain why Iapetus looks this way. One theory is that dark material blows from the next outermost moon, Phoebe, due to meteoroid impacts. The dark material then falls toward Saturn. Since Iapetus is between Phoebe and Saturn, it might sweep up some of this material. But no one has confirmed this.

Iapetus had some other surprises waiting for the *Voyager* researchers, notably the mountain range on Iapetus's equator. The ridge is an almost perfectly straight line and makes the moon look something like a walnut, or as though Iapetus were made in two halves that were squashed together. The mountain range is at least 800 miles (1,300 km) long, wrapping one-third of the way around the moon. The peaks of the range are up to 8 miles (13 km) high, 3 miles (5 km) higher than the highest mountains on Earth, which is impressive for a moon only 914 miles (1,471 km) wide. No one knows what formed this weird-looking mountain range. Several ideas have been proposed. One of the most popular is that Iapetus once had a ring of debris circling it. Eventually, all of this debris fell, bit by bit, onto the moon. Because of the low gravity, it landed on the surface at a fairly low speed. Instead of

The stark divide between the black and white areas on Iapetus would make for incredible landscapes for any visitors.

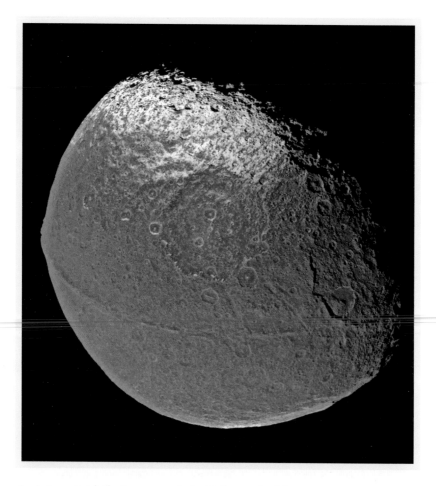

Iapetus's equatorial ridge is easy to see in *Cassini* photographs of the moon.

creating craters or vaporizing in explosions, the material gradually piled up into a long, straight mountain range exactly on the moon's equator.

TETHYS

Tethys is one of Saturn's larger moons. It is about 660 miles (1,066 km) wide and made almost entirely of ice. Future space tourists may visit Tethys to view one of the most impressive canyons in the solar system. This canyon, Ithaca Chasma, is about 60 miles (100 km) wide and more than 1,200 miles (2,000 km) long, wrapping two-thirds of the way around the little moon. Ithaca Chasma is really a graben, a geological feature that is created when a block of a planet or moon's crust is displaced downward. The result is a valley with a nearly flat floor and steep sides. Ithaca Chasma might have been created at the same time as a giant impact crater on the other side of Tethys. Odysseus Crater would be worth a visit all by itself. At 250 miles (400 km) wide, the crater spreads across nearly two-fifths of the surface of Tethys. Because the crater is so large and Tethys is so small, you would not be able to see one side of the crater from the other.

MIMAS

Every planet and moon in the solar system has been hit by a meteoroid or an asteroid at some time—usually many thousands of times. The gas giants don't show any evidence of this bombardment because they are made of gas and liquid. An asteroid crashing into a planet like Jupiter or Saturn would no more leave a crater than a stone dropped into a pond would leave a hole in the water. But the solid worlds, like the solar system's moons, have many craters—some of them extremely large. The largest crater on Earth's moon, for instance, is called the South Pole-Aitken basin and is 1,600 miles (2,575 km) wide and 8.1 miles (13 km) deep, almost as wide as the Atlantic Ocean.

Another moon with a giant crater is Mimas, a satellite of Saturn. Herschel is such a large crater that Mimas was almost destroyed by the impact that created it. The crater is 81 miles (130 km) wide. While not nearly as large as the largest crater on Earth's moon, it takes up almost one-third the diameter of Mimas, which is only 247 miles (397 km) wide. If Earth had a proportionally large crater of its own, the crater would be as wide as the United States.

The view from Herschel would be one of the most spectacular in the solar system. If you were standing on the rim, the 3-mile-high (5 km) crater walls would look like great cliffs curving off into the

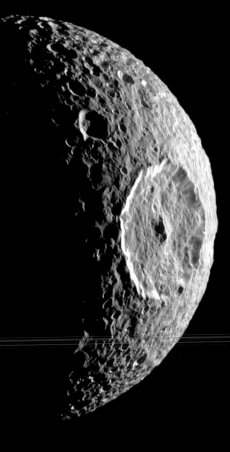

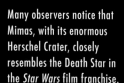
Many observers notice that Mimas, with its enormous Herschel Crater, closely resembles the Death Star in the *Star Wars* film franchise.

distance. The floor of the crater would be more than 6 miles (10 km) below your feet. The towering central peak would dominate your view. It is 3.7 miles (6 km) high, almost as high as Mount Everest. But overwhelming everything would be Saturn itself. The giant planet is only 115,000 miles (185,075 km) away, less than half the distance separating Earth from the Moon. Saturn is so much bigger than our moon that it would look seventy-two times larger than a full moon does in the night sky of Earth. It would fill the sky above Herschel.

PAN AND ATLAS

At only 8.8 miles (14 km) wide, Pan is an extremely tiny moon of Saturn. It orbits within the 200-mile-wide (325 km) Encke Gap

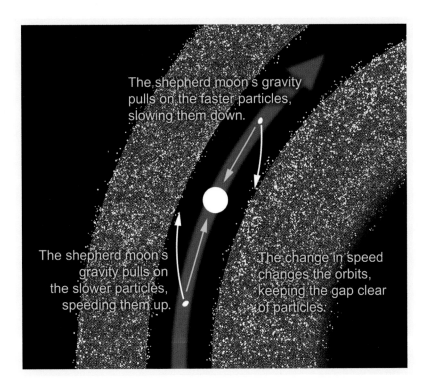

The shepherd moon's gravity pulls on the faster particles, slowing them down.

The shepherd moon's gravity pulls on the slower particles, speeding them up.

The change in speed changes the orbits, keeping the gap clear of particles.

When ring particles are slowed down or sped up by a shepherd moon, they move to lower or higher orbits around the planet, respectively, due to the laws of angular momentum.

of Saturn's A ring. Orbiting Saturn every 13.8 hours, Pan acts as a shepherd moon, keeping the Encke Gap swept clear. Like the many other shepherd moons, Pan creates a "wake" on either side as it orbits within the ring material. The moon's gravity will slow down ring particles ahead of the moon, causing them to move into lower orbit closer to the planet, and speed up particles that are behind the moon, causing them to move into a higher orbit farther from the planet. The moon clears the path of the shepherd ring, creating a gap.

Shepherd moons also help to maintain the gaps in the ring by collecting dust and debris like tiny vacuum cleaners, constantly adding material to their mass and gradually growing a little larger. This effect might help explain a mystery about Pan and its near twin, Atlas, which orbits at the outer edge of the A ring.

URANUS'S SHEPHERD MOONS

Although Uranus's ring system is not nearly as spectacular as Saturn's, the planet also has a pair of shepherd moons. Cordelia is a fast-orbiting satellite on the inside of the planet's brightest ring. Like Pan and Atlas, it is too small to be affected by the planet's Roche limit. Its gravity speeds up dust particles and nudges them into a higher orbit. Cordelia's slower-moving sister, Ophelia, orbits on the outside of the same ring and slows down particles, shepherding them into a lower orbit. Together, Cordelia and Ophelia have herded the particles of dust and ice into a narrow, sharp-edged ring between them.

What makes Pan and Atlas mysterious is not their jobs as ring shepherds but their strange shapes. They look like classic flying saucers or perhaps overstuffed cheeseburgers. Like no other moons anywhere else in the solar system, these two have prominent equatorial ridges. The origins of these bulges are unknown, but some scientists think they may be from ring material building up around the moons' equators as they sweep up tiny particles of ice and dust. These little moons can exist within Saturn's Roche limit without being broken to pieces because they are so small. The effect of such tidal forces depends on the difference in gravitational pull between the side of an object nearer a planet and the side farther away. A large moon approaching too close to a planet will be torn apart because the effect of gravity on its opposite sides would be so extreme. But tiny moons such as Pan and Atlas are immune because of their small size. The ice they are made of is stronger than the difference in gravitational pull between opposite sides.

MINOR-PLANET MOONS

Not every moon orbits a planet. Even asteroids can have moons of their own. Size seems to be no restriction, with asteroids less than 1 mile (1.6 km) wide possessing even tinier moons. The first asteroid discovered to have a moon is Ida, a 9-mile-wide (15 km) rock in the asteroid belt. Photos taken in 1993 by the *Galileo* spacecraft revealed that Ida was accompanied by a miniature moon. The moon, Dactyl, is less than a mile wide. Since the discovery of Dactyl, astronomers have found that nearly 360 asteroids have moons of their own.

An even bigger surprise came in 2005 when astronomers discovered that the asteroid Sylvia had *two* moons, making it the first known triple-asteroid system. Several other triple systems have been discovered since.

MOONS BEYOND THE SOLAR SYSTEM

In 1998 astronomers discovered an extrasolar planet, or exoplanet: a planet orbiting a star other than the sun. Since then, more than four thousand exoplanets have been discovered. At first, only very large exoplanets—the size of Jupiter or even larger—could be observed, but as equipment and techniques improved, astronomers were able to detect much smaller exoplanets. Nearly sixty exoplanets about the size of Earth are known to exist. From the discovery of the first exoplanet, scientists wondered if any of them might have moons. Since most

FINDING EXOMOONS

The Hunt for Exomoons with Kepler project, affiliated with the Harvard-Smithsonian Center for Astrophysics, aims to use the Kepler Space Telescope to discover moons orbiting distant exoplanets. Scientists are using two methods to detect possible moons.

As a planet orbits a star, it will transit, or pass between the star and an observer. During a transit, light from the star is dimmed slightly as the planet passes in front of it. If a moon is orbiting the planet, then the dimming of the star will change slightly during the transit because the exomoon may transit the star before or just after the planet does.

Another method for detecting an exomoon is to look for changes in the time it takes a planet to transit a star. As a moon orbits a planet, it tugs on it, causing the planet to shift back and forth. This will affect the timing of a transit, making it shorter or longer than if the planet had no moon.

planets in our solar system have at least one moon, astronomers assume that exoplanets have moons too. But finding something as tiny as a moon would be even more difficult than discovering planets as small as Earth.

The first exomoon thought to be discovered was not very small. In 2018 astronomers David Kipping and Alex Teachey, examining data from the Hubble and Kepler Space Telescopes, believed that the Jupiter-sized exoplanet Kepler-1625b possessed a moon the size of Neptune. But whether this moon really exists is debatable. Some astronomers believe that due to the difficulty in detecting the effects of an exomoon on an exoplanet's transit, what Kipping and Teachey found may be simply noise in the data.

In 2019 Italian astronomer Cecelia Lazzoni was examining a red dwarf star. She found a body ten to eleven times the size of Jupiter orbiting it. It is so large that it may not technically be a planet. It may be a brown dwarf, an object not quite small enough to be a planet and not quite large enough to trigger the nuclear reaction needed to become a full-fledged star. A brown dwarf may even glow a dim red, like a dying coal. This strange planet orbits the red dwarf at a distance of about ten times the distance of Earth from the sun. Circling it is a moon slightly smaller than Jupiter. Later that year, Lazzoni found another red dwarf star with a planet 11 to 14 times the size of Jupiter with a moon about 4.6 times the size of Jupiter.

Are these really moons? If the exoplanets turn out to be brown dwarfs, then they may be more a star than a planet, and moons do not orbit stars. But if the exoplanets turn out to be true planets, then the first exomoons may have been found.

One reason scientists are anxious to prove the existence of exomoons is that it widens the possibilities for life in the universe. An exoplanet similar to Jupiter with an environment too hostile for life to evolve might be orbited by a moon the size of Earth, where conditions may be much more conducive to life.

9

ABODES FOR LIFE?

For more than a century, the search for life elsewhere in the solar system has been focused on Mars. For many scientists, Mars was the most obvious place to look for extraterrestrial life. Venus and Mercury are much too close to the sun and much too hot to support life, while the outer planets are very cold and covered with poisonous gases. While Mars is cold too, and has only a very thin atmosphere, it once had oceans and seas made of water, just like those on Earth. Although Mars's oceans vanished billions of years ago, a lot of water is left as ice buried just beneath the surface. Even if life no longer exists on Mars, it may have at one time and left behind fossil remnants.

The focus on Mars began to change when scientists made some startling discoveries in the early twenty-first century. The most important was the discovery that one or more of Jupiter's icy moons might possess vast underground seas of warm, liquid water. Even more intriguing, these oceans appeared to be rich in organic chemical compounds known to be the among the basic building blocks of life.

FOLLOW THE WATER

The search for life in the solar system is aligned with the search for water. With very few exceptions, life as we know it depends on the existence of liquid water. Three factors combined on the early Earth, some four billion years ago, to kick-start the formation of life: liquid water, the right chemicals, and a source of energy. For a long time, experts assumed that energy source was sunlight—with perhaps an added boost from lightning or asteroid or meteoroid impacts.

An experiment first performed in 1953 by scientists Stanley Miller and Harold Urey gave a lot of credence to this theory. A sealed container was filled with a mixture of water, ammonia, methane, and hydrogen: the components of Earth's early atmosphere. An electric spark was used to simulate lightning. The result was the formation of complex amino acids and other organic molecules, the basic building blocks of life. In the early history of Earth, these building blocks combined in further reactions, each time forming larger, more complex molecules, such as proteins and nucleic acids. Many scientists believe that eventually these complex molecules formed the first cells, and thus the first forms of life.

Besides having all the right ingredients for the evolution of life, Earth had two additional important qualities, a dense atmosphere and a magnetic field. Both of these helped shield the surface of the planet from dangerous solar radiation that would not only be deadly to any early forms of life but also would prevent complex molecules from forming in the first place by breaking up the bonds between the atoms. Most of the solar system's moons do not have the protection provided by an atmosphere and a magnetic field. And because they have no atmospheres in which lightning can occur and are so far from the sun, they lack the sources of energy that supported Earth's early life. Ice, however, addresses all of these problems.

Many of the solar system's large moons are made primarily of water ice. Because of the heating effect created by tidal flexing, ice deep beneath the surfaces of these moons not only has melted but remains warm. The warm water would have dissolved all the right chemicals to form organic compounds: ammonia, methane, hydrogen, and more. Although the ice blocks most of the sunlight that reaches these moons, the tidal heating within the planet provides a source of energy. Solid ice many miles thick is also a very good shield against dangerous radiation. So, with all the necessary ingredients—warm liquid water, the right chemicals, a source of energy, billions of years, and a radiation shield—life may have evolved in those dark, hidden seas. While many of the solar system's icy moons may have warm liquid water beneath their icy crusts, scientists are focusing their attention on three main candidates for the existence of life: Europa, Enceladus, and Titan.

EUROPA

Europa was the first moon that astronomers suspected harbored a hidden ocean. When the *Voyager 1* and *Voyager 2* spacecraft flew past Jupiter in 1979, the photographs they sent back to Earth of Europa showed that Europa was covered with a thick layer of ice. Astronomers wondered if the ice might be floating atop a deep ocean of liquid water.

Seen from space, Europa's surface closely resembles ice floes in the Arctic and Antarctic, giant blocks of ice that are continuously breaking apart and colliding. On Earth the movement of floes happens because the ice is floating on seas of liquid water. Could the same thing be occurring on Europa?

Scientists would not know the answer until the *Galileo* orbiter arrived at the Jupiter system in 1995. Besides studying the giant planet, the orbiter also made flybys of several of Jupiter's moons, including Europa. Measurements made by *Galileo* confirmed the scientists' suspicions. The thick, icy crust of Europa is floating on top of a deep layer of salty water, kept warm in liquid form by the tidal forces created by Jupiter. Scientists suspect that the bottom of the ocean contains

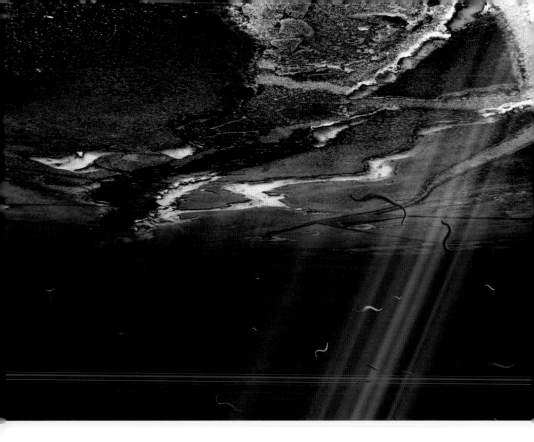

This illustration of the subsurface ocean on Europa shows strange life forms swimming under a particularly thin section of ice.

geothermal features, such as underwater hot springs and geysers, where warm, mineral-rich water is constantly flowing into the sea.

But was there any more direct evidence of this hidden ocean? One clue would be if some of that ocean were leaking into space, perhaps as geysers jetting from cracks in the surface ice. Scientists had the *Galileo* orbiter search for plumes of ice crystals but with no luck. However, observations by the Hubble Space Telescope have suggested that thin wisps of water are being ejected as high as 100 miles (160 km) above the surface of Europa. In late 2019, a team of astronomers announced that they had successfully detected water vapor above the surface of the moon. This confirmed the existence of either one or several oceans beneath Europa's ice.

ON TO SATURN

The other two moons where scientists hope to search for life belong to Saturn. The *Cassini* spacecraft explored Saturn and several of its moons, orbiting the planet from 2005 to 2017. *Cassini* was a collaboration between NASA, the European Space Agency, and the Italian space agency, Agenzia Spaziale Italiana. Besides collecting data about Saturn and taking hundreds of photos of the planet, *Cassini* flew past Enceladus, sending dozens of close-up photos of the little moon back to Earth. The spacecraft also carried the *Huygens*, which parachuted to the surface of Saturn's largest moon, Titan, in January 2005. Both of these moons were filled with surprises.

ENCELADUS

Enceladus is bright. It is the brightest of all the moons and planets because it is covered in icy, snowlike dust. It orbits in the middle of the E ring, a thin, faint ring of tiny ice particles surrounding Saturn. Scientists wondered where all of these ice particles came from. They detected chemical compounds in the E ring that resembled the composition of the ice on Enceladus. It was evident that the ice in the ring came from Enceladus, but scientists were unsure how the ice left the moon and entered orbit around Saturn. One hypothesis was that Enceladus was somehow emitting water vapor or ice. If so, how was it doing this, and how did it replenish the material it was sending into space? Was there some hidden source for the water and ice?

Enceladus orbits so close to Saturn that it is within the planet's magnetic field. When *Cassini* flew past the little moon in 2005, its instruments discovered some mysterious disturbances in the field above Enceladus's southern polar regions. This indicated that instead of being a dead, frozen ball of ice, Enceladus was an active world. Something was going on inside it.

Although a few scientists had long suspected that Enceladus might possess cryogeysers, there was no proof until *Cassini* made its first close

Astronomers think Enceladus's south pole geysers may exist due to the heating of subsurface reservoirs of water.

pass by the moon. One of the first photos sent back to Earth astonished scientists. Instead of a frozen, airless ball of ice, Enceladus looked more like a comet. Giant, feathery plumes of ice crystals swirled above the moon's southern polar regions.

Cassini's photos revealed that powerful geysers are constantly erupting from cracks in the surface of Enceladus. These jets consist of water and organic chemicals and shoot hundreds of miles into space at 800 miles (1,287 km) an hour. Some of this material falls back onto Enceladus as snow. The rest of the ice joins Saturn's E ring.

When the *Cassini* spacecraft flew through one of the icy plumes, it detected that the plumes were made of not only water and organic molecules, including carbon dioxide and carbon monoxide, but also tiny grains of silica. Scientists knew that this particular form of silica could only be created when water and rock interact at temperatures above 200°F (93°C). The presence of this mineral pointed to the existence of hydrothermal vents in the floor of Enceladus's ocean, similar to the hydrothermal vents in certain areas of the bottom of

Earth's ocean. Hydrothermal vents are underwater hot springs, where boiling water—mixed with all sorts of dissolved minerals—erupts through fissures. Scientists are certain that a body of warm, liquid water about 6 miles (10 km) deep is beneath the southern polar region of Enceladus, under an ice shell 19 to 25 miles (30 to 40 km) thick.

EXTREMOPHILES

One place on Earth resembles some of the conditions deep within Enceladus's ocean. In 1977 scientists exploring the Pacific Ocean floor near the Galápagos Islands off the coast of Ecuador discovered vents of superheated, mineral-rich water at a depth of 8,000 feet (2,438 m). The water coming from the vents was 700°F (371°C), more than three times hotter than the temperature of boiling water at sea level. The intense pressure at such a great depth keeps the water from instantly turning to steam. The vents themselves look like chimneys, reaching as high as 180 feet (55 m) above the ocean floor. These chimneys are created by deposits of the minerals—sulfur, iron, zinc, copper, lead, and cobalt—that the hot water dissolves.

The discovery of these vents was amazing enough, but the scientists were astounded to find that the area around the vents was home to previously unknown organisms that somehow thrived despite the absence of sunlight, the intense heat, and the mineral-laden water. Life could still exist under conditions that would be lethal to almost all other types of life on Earth. A complex ecosystem had evolved surrounding the vents, based on a food chain that began with microbes that thrived on the minerals in the hot water. Instead of relying on photosynthesis to generate energy like terrestrial plants, these bacteria use chemicals such as hydrogen sulfide as their energy source. The bacteria in turn feed an increasingly complex chain of organisms, such as shrimp and tube worms, all unique to the environment surrounding the vents.

When scientists first suspected the existence of oceans and seas beneath the icy crusts of Europa and Enceladus, they were immediately reminded of the conditions that exist around the hydrothermal vents at the bottom of Earth's oceans. Plumes of water ice rich in organic hydrocarbons, a large salty ocean, and warm hydrothermal vents on the seafloor are all signs that Enceladus might be one of the most promising—if most unexpected—abodes for life in the solar system.

TITAN

Titan is the only moon in the solar system known to have a substantial atmosphere. And it is the only place besides Earth known to have liquids in the form of rivers, lakes, and seas on its surface. The largest of Titan's seas are hundreds of feet deep and hundreds of miles wide. The liquids contained in these bodies are not water, however, but rather methane and ethane at temperatures hundreds of degrees below the freezing point of water. What water is for Earth, these liquids are for Titan: methane rains fall from methane clouds, and methane rivers

The bottom of Enceladus's seas may feature hydrothermal vents releasing hot, mineral-laden water and gases.

flow into methane lakes and seas where the methane evaporates back into the atmosphere to start the cycle again.

The crust of Titan is mostly water ice. About 120 miles (200 km) beneath this lies an ocean of liquid water kept warm by the slow decay of radioactive elements deep within the moon's core. This ocean may be as deep as 140 to 185 miles (225 to 300 km). Powered by the core's heat, ice volcanoes and ice geysers erupt on the surface of Titan, where warm water—mixed with methane and other organic compounds—escapes into the atmosphere or flows over the landscape in streams and rivers.

Titan has everything that life needs to get started. The chances of life having evolved in its underground ocean are as good as those for Europa and Enceladus. But what about life on its surface? On other ice moons, there is little or no protection from solar radiation and cosmic rays. Europa and Enceladus don't have magnetic fields or dense atmospheres like those that shield the surface of Earth from these dangers. Titan doesn't have a magnetic field, either, but it has a dense nitrogen atmosphere. Its atmosphere is 60 percent denser than Earth's and more than sufficient to protect the surface of the moon from radiation.

LIFE WITHOUT WATER

If life exists at all on Titan, it would have to be something very alien to anything we know on Earth. There is no oxygen in Titan's atmosphere and very little carbon dioxide. And a surface temperature of –290°F (–179°C) would prevent any possibility of liquid water existing. The structure of the DNA molecule, which is the foundation of all life on our planet, requires oxygen and liquid water, neither of which are very abundant on Titan. One of the main functions of water for life on Earth is to act as a solvent. Almost everything can dissolve in water, so it is vital for carrying chemicals and chemical compounds and helping them combine into new forms. However, many hydrocarbons, such as methane and ethane, can also act as solvents over a wide range of temperatures. These might take the place of water, dissolving and transporting the necessary chemical components of life.

Life on Titan would be part of an ecosystem based on methane rather than water. Instead of being composed mostly of carbon and water, like life on Earth, life on Titan would be made up mostly of carbon, hydrogen, methane, and ethane. Organisms would not inhale oxygen as humans do or carbon dioxide as plants do on Earth. Instead, they might breathe or absorb methane or ethane. And instead of releasing carbon dioxide as people do or oxygen as plants do, they would release hydrogen, which would combine with nitrogen to form hydrocarbon molecules in the atmosphere.

Titan's atmosphere of thick clouds blocks most of the sunlight that reaches the moon, so the surface is very dark. Like creatures that live in lightless caverns on Earth, life on Titan—whether plant or animal— might be unpigmented. But dark colors might help life-forms absorb what little energy from the sun manages to penetrate the clouds. This might mean that life on Titan is dark red, purple, or even black, like many of the creatures that live deep in Earth's oceans.

The gravity on Titan is also about one-seventh the strength of Earth's gravity, so any animals on Titan could get by with much thinner, lighter skeletons. The very dense atmosphere would make it much easier for any birdlike creatures to fly. Or perhaps there might even be living balloons, inflated with the hydrogen gas they create.

Future explorers may discover something living on Titan's surface—perhaps huddled near the relative warmth of a hot spring— that is unlike anything that exists on our planet.

SEARCHING FOR LIFE

Exploring ordinary moons is relatively straightforward compared to exploring a moon that might harbor life. Most of the solar system's moons are airless balls of rock or ice. An explorer would land, take some pictures, gather some samples, and leave. But the moons that

Weather on Titan, such as this dust storm, may produce lightning, which could potentially spark life in the organic material on the moon's surface.

scientists suspect of having evolved some form of life present special problems. Some have atmospheres that make landing on them difficult. A probe meant to land on Titan would have to navigate through an opaque blanket of clouds and then parachute to a landing. It would be hard to make a pinpoint landing on an ideal spot during an unexpected gust of wind. The probe might end up toppled over on the side of a hill, stuck at the bottom of a ravine, or sunk in one of Titan's lakes. Probes visiting worlds like Europa or Enceladus face a different challenge: getting through a crust of ice many miles thick to reach the seas buried beneath, which is difficult even for scientists exploring the ice caps of our own planet. Despite these obstacles, space agencies are planning for future explorations of Enceladus, Europa, and Titan.

NASA has proposed designs for orbiters that would take samples from the plumes of Enceladus's cryogeysers. One such orbiter might be part of the Enceladus Life Finder (ELF) mission, which would search for signs of organic molecules in the plumes, looking for amino acids, methane, and other substances that might be signatures of life.

Meanwhile, the German Aerospace Center has proposed the Enceladus Explorer, which would land a station on the surface of the moon not far from one of the cryogeyser vents. It would then deploy the IceMole, a probe that would melt its way at least 656 feet (200 m) into the ice, looking for signs of microorganisms along the way.

Europa Lander is a mission being designed by NASA that would send a spacecraft able to gather samples and examine them in a built-in laboratory. The spacecraft may even be equipped with a drill that could take samples from about 4 inches (10 cm) beneath the surface.

An even more ambitious idea has been proposed for a mission in the distant future: launching a submarine into Europa's hidden ocean. Such a mission would face many challenges. First, the submarine has to get through at least 6 miles (10 km) of solid ice, a problem that scientists aren't sure how to solve. Additionally, the submarine probe needs to be designed so that it could operate entirely on its own, automatically recording everything it finds for later transmission to the surface. Undeterred by these difficulties, some NASA engineers have taken the first steps in developing such a probe. In 2015 a prototype called Artemis was tested in Antarctic waters. At 14 feet (4.2 m) long and weighing over 2,800 pounds (1,270 kg), Artemis was able to travel a little over 3 miles (5 km) under the Antarctic ice on its own before returning to its drop-off point and automatically docking. Though far too big and heavy for an actual mission to Europa, Artemis is the first step in demonstrating that such a project may be possible.

Researchers think the best way to get through the ice shell of Europa's surface is to melt a hole, possibly with a special probe powered by a nuclear reactor. Heat from the reactor might be used directly in melting the ice, or it might power a set of lasers that would do the melting. Initial tests of a laser-boring device on a glacier in Alaska have been successful, penetrating about 72 feet (22 m) of ice in an hour.

In 2019 NASA began tests in Antarctica of a new type of rover meant for the exploration of Europa. The Buoyant Rover for Under-Ice Exploration (BRUIE) would work a little like an upside-down rover. Instead of crawling around on top of Europa's ice floes, it would crawl around under them. BRUIE would consist of a 3-foot-long (1 m) package of instruments with two large wheels at either end. The entire rover would be lighter than water, so its buoyancy would keep it pressed against the underside of the ice. Gear-like teeth around the rims of the wheels would grip the ice and enable BRUIE to move around.

As with most plans for exploring the sea beneath Europa's icy crust, a lot depends on knowing how thick that layer is. If it is too thick, it might be impossible to penetrate. The Europa Clipper mission will send a spacecraft will orbit Europa, searching for safe sites for landers and measuring the depth of Europa's ice to see if projects such as BRUIE would be possible.

The Titan Mare Explorer would splash down in one of Titan's methane lakes, where it would float for at least two Titan days (equivalent to sixteen Earth days), gathering information and samples. It would be able to determine the exact composition of Titan's lakes, looking for complex hydrocarbons that might be a telltale sign of life—or at least a sign that the basic components of life exist there. A robot submarine has also been proposed for exploring the seas of Titan. It would be able to cruise on the surface as well as dive to great depths.

Perhaps the most ambitious project is NASA's *Dragonfly*, a robotic drone the size of a Mars rover that could explore Titan by air. With a planned launch in 2026, it would fly from place to place, recording images and data along the way and taking samples from wherever it lands. In two and half years it would cover over 100 miles (175 km) of Titan's surface. Its main goal will be to explore the crater Selk, where

About 3 feet (1 m) across, *Dragonfly* can fly at 22.4 miles (36 km) per hour in Titan's low gravity. Because of Titan's thick atmosphere, *Dragonfly*'s rechargeable battery will not be solar powered like those of many other spacecraft, but rather will produce electricity from the decay of radioactive material.

scientists believe it has the best chance of finding conditions similar to those that existed when life first appeared on Earth.

Thanks to these missions, astronomers will begin to understand even more about our own solar system. The search for extraterrestrial life is only one aspect of the research that astronomers are undertaking as they study the solar system's moons. Some of the moons may answer our questions about the origins of the solar system, while others may contain secrets we have yet to realize. No longer are they considered mere lumps of unimportant rock. Moons have become the subject of prolific research and hotbeds of scientific discovery.

GLOSSARY

accretion: the process by which larger bodies in space grow from the accumulation of smaller ones

ammonia (NH_3): a poisonous compound of nitrogen and hydrogen

asteroid: any one of the thousands of small, rocky-metallic bodies, ranging from a few hundred feet to about 500 miles (806 km) across, that orbit the sun

astronaut: a human space explorer

astronomer: a scientist who studies objects and phenomena in outer space

caldera: a large, usually flat-bottomed crater with straight, steep sides created when a volcano collapses

carbon dioxide (CO_2): a colorless, odorless gas that is a compound of carbon and oxygen

corona: the outermost region of the sun's atmosphere

crater: a hole created in a planet or moon by the impact of an asteroid or meteoroid

cryogeyser: a geyser that erupts cold water and ices

cryovolcano: a volcano that erupts cold water and ices

eclipse: an event when a planet or moon passes through the shadow of another celestial body

evolution: the process by which living organisms gradually develop and diversify from earlier forms

farside: the side of Earth's moon that is permanently facing away from Earth

fumarole: a small volcanic vent in the surface of a planet or moon that emits hot steam and other gases

Galilean moons: the four largest moons of Jupiter, named for their discoverer, Galileo Galilei

gravity: the force by which all masses attract all other masses

greenhouse gas: a material that traps heat in the atmosphere of a planet by absorbing infrared radiation given off by the planet's surface

hydrocarbon: any organic compound consisting entirely of hydrogen and carbon

hydrogen (H): the simplest, lightest, and most common element in the universe

irregular moon: a moon that orbits its planet in a very different way from the planet's other moons

Kuiper Belt: the region of the solar system extending beyond the orbit of Neptune and containing icy bodies

mare: a dark, smooth area on the Moon's surface where ancient lava once flowed. Maria is the plural form.

mass: the amount of material in an object

mesa: a flat-topped hill or mountain

meteoroid: an interplanetary rock or metal body smaller than an asteroid

methane (CH_4): a compound of hydrogen and carbon

moon: any small body orbiting another, larger one; also the natural satellite that orbits Earth

nearside: the side of the Moon that faces Earth

orbit: the path an object follows when moving around another one

penitente: formations of ice taking the form of tall, slender peaks or blades

phase: the differing appearance of the Moon as it circles Earth, caused by the changing angle of the sunlight illuminating the Moon

planetesimal: any small body—from a few inches to a few feet in size—from which planets are eventually formed

precession: the slow wobble in Earth's axis as the planet spins

protoplanetary disk: the disk of dust surrounding a star from which planets may eventually form

protostar: a gravitationally stable cloud of dust that is massive enough to eventually form into a star

retrograde: the motion of a planet or moon in a direction opposite to that of other bodies within its system

revolution: the movement of one body around another

rill: a type of lunar valley

Roche limit: the minimum distance a moon can orbit a planet with being torn apart by tidal forces. It is also the minimum distance from a planet that a moon could form.

rotation: the spinning of a body on its axis

satellite: any small body orbiting another, larger one

scarp: a steep slope or cliff created when one crustal plate lifts above another one

selenography: the science of studying the Moon

silica: another name for silicon dioxide (SiO_2). On Earth, it is often found in minerals such as quartz, flint, or agate.

solar system: the sun and all the bodies orbiting it

sublimation: when a solid turns into a gas without first becoming a liquid

synestia: the hot cloud of gas and dust from which Earth and the Moon formed

tectonic: relating to the movement of continental plates

telescope: an instrument consisting of a series of lenses and sometimes mirrors that allows distant objects to be seen clearly

tidal flexing: a process in which the gravity of a nearby body stretches or squeezes an astronomical object, producing heat

tide: a bulge raised in a body by the gravitational force of a nearby body

SOURCE NOTES

9   George Gamow, *Biography of Physics* (New York: Harper Torchbooks, 1961), 16.

20 Galileo Galilei, *Discoveries and Opinions of Galileo: Including the Starry Messenger (1610), Letter to the Grand Duchess Christina (1615), and Excerpts from Letters on Sunspots (1613), The Assayer (1623)*, ed. Stillman Drake (New York: Doubleday, 1957), 31.

34 Galilei, 51.

34 Galilei, 53.

SELECTED BIBLIOGRAPHY

Batson, Raymond M. Voyager 1 *and* 2 *Atlas of Six Saturnian Satellites*. Washington, DC: NASA, 1984.

Beatty, J. Kelly, Carolyn Collins Peterson, and Andrew Chaikin. *The New Solar System*. Cambridge, MA: Sky, 1999.

Boyce, Joseph M. *Our Solar System*. Washington, DC: NASA, 1992.

Burns, Joseph A., and Mildred Shapley Matthews. *Satellites*. Tucson: University of Arizona Press, 1986.

Faure, Gunter, and Teresa M. Mensing. *Introduction to Planetary Science*. Dordrecht, Netherlands: Springer, 2007.

Harley, Timothy. *Moon Lore*. Rutland, VT: Charles E. Tuttle, 1970.

Hartmann, William K. *Astronomy: The Cosmic Journey*. Belmont, CA: Wadsworth, 1985.

———. *Moons & Planets*. Belmont, CA: Wadsworth, 1999

Kohlhase, Charles. *The Voyager Neptune Travel Guide*. Washington, DC: NASA, 1989.

Miller, Ron, and William K. Hartmann. *The Grand Tour*. New York: Workman, 2005.

Spilker, Linda J. *Passage to a Ringed World*. Washington, DC: NASA, 1997.

Stern, Alan, and Jacqueline Mitton. *Pluto and Charon*. Weinheim, Germany: Wiley-VCH, 2005.

FURTHER INFORMATION

BOOKS

Hand, Kevin. *Alien Oceans: The Search for Life in the Depths of Space*. Princeton, NJ: Princeton University Press, 2020.

Kenney, Karen Latchana. *Exoplanets: Worlds beyond Our Solar System*. Minneapolis: Twenty-First Century Books, 2017.

Lorenz, Ralph. *Saturn's Moon Titan Owners' Workshop Manual*. Sparkford, UK: Haynes, 2020.

Meltzer, Michael. *Mission to Jupiter*. Washington, DC: NASA, 2012.

Miller, Ron. *Seven Wonders of the Gas Giants and Their Moons*. Minneapolis: Twenty-First Century Books, 2011.

———. *Seven Wonders of the Rocky Planets and Their Moons*. Minneapolis: Twenty-First Century Books, 2011.

NASA. *The Saturn System through the Eyes of Cassini*. Washington, DC: 12th Media Services, 2018.

Read, John A. *50 Things to See on the Moon: A First-Time Stargazer's Guide*. Halifax, Nova Scotia, Canada: Formac, 2019.

WEBSITES

Astronomy Magazine
https://astronomy.com/
Astronomy publishes the latest news in astronomical discoveries.

Earth's Moon
https://solarsystem.nasa.gov/moons/earths-moon/in-depth/
This NASA page is devoted to the latest findings about Earth's moon.

Europa Missions
https://www.jpl.nasa.gov/missions/?search=&type=&missions_target=Europa&mission_type=&launch_date=#submit
Visit the Jet Propulsion Laboratory, a part of NASA, to learn about future missions to Europa.

The Jet Propulsion Laboratory Photojournal
https://photojournal.jpl.nasa.gov/
This NASA site contains thousands of images of Earth's moon and the moons of other planets.

Jupiter's Moons
https://solarsystem.nasa.gov/missions/galileo/overview/
This NASA site is devoted to the *Galileo* orbiter, which orbited Jupiter from 1995 to 2003.

Mars's Moons
https://mars.nasa.gov/mro/
This NASA site publishes updates on the *Mars Reconnaissance Orbiter*, a spacecraft that has been in orbit around Mars since 2006.

Moons in the Solar System
https://theplanets.org/moons/
Learn the basic facts about the moons of the solar system, including size and orbital distance from the parent planet.

"Moon Size Comparison." YouTube video, 4:59. Posted by Red Side, January 21, 2019. https://www.youtube.com/watch?v=LMuGpkIbp5s/.
This video proceeds from the smallest moon in the solar system to the largest, showing their sizes to scale.

Other Moons
https://solarsystem.nasa.gov/moons/overview/
This NASA site describes the different moons of the solar system.

Saturn's Moons
http://www.ciclops.org/
Visit the official website for images from the Cassini–Huygens mission to get a close look at Saturn and its moons.

Space.com
https://www.space.com/
Read news about space exploration and astronomy from this accessible online publication.

INDEX

ABOUT THE AUTHOR

Ron Miller is the award-winning author and illustrator of more than sixty books. In addition to the art he creates for his own books, Miller has illustrated dozens of others, including the best-selling *Zoomable Universe*. He is also a regular contributor of art to magazines such as *Astronomy* and *Scientific American*, has been a production designer and illustrator on films such as *Dune* (1984) and *Comet Impact* (2000), and has been a member of the NASA Fine Arts Program. Miller's Pluto postage stamp, attached to the *New Horizons* spacecraft, has now traveled farther than any stamp in postal history.

PHOTO ACKNOWLEDGMENTS